Zebras are Magic...

Zebras are Magic...

and other everyday absurdities

Written By:
Sharon T. Meitin

Cover Design By:
kelly@kellybryantdesign.com

ISBN: 1539574636
ISBN 13: 9781539574637

This book is dedicated to myself because I wrote it,
and to all the birds that helped me finish it.

Introduction

Read this book instead of watching the news and you'll be glad you did. I hope you enjoy it.

Table of Contents

CHAPTER 1

*Illegal Alien

I spent my freshman year at an all-women's college. "Good Lord Why?" You ask. Well, I chose "Girl College" based on the result of a very sophisticated process: I visited the campus in high school, saw the best social scene available and that was enough to sell me. Thrilled I had the opportunity to attend what was once her dream college, Mom happily guided me through the application process. I should have noticed her card catalog of preferred schools resourced 1950's Irish Catholic Chicago. Options were a bit limited back then; a girl could attend The University of Illinois if she was smart enough, a local college for teaching or nursing, trade school for court reporting, paralegal training and the like. All were very respectable paths, but to Mom, Girl College was the crown jewel and a vicariously attainable one at that. It offered a quality Liberal Arts education and if lucky, a "M-r-s." degree with a minor in eternal happiness from its nearby brother university.

Because my printing was so atrocious, Mom physically filled out the application as I dictated answers to complicated questions like:

Name, Address and *Name of High School.* All applicants had to write an essay on "A Woman Who Influences You the Most" and I don't think 5 minutes passed before she began to intensely write. Who was I to stop her from pursuing her dream, even if by proxy? A couple days later, she interrupted my viewing of a "very special" *Family Ties* to tell me that she wrote my essay on *Barbara Bush* and mailed it for me because otherwise, I "would have never done it." I was not surprised considering she wrote my "Mayor for a Day" paper in 7th grade. I think she saw it as an opportunity to gripe about city operations rather than just complain publicly. Part of the paper focused on the overgrown trees that obstructed her vision while driving - because 13-year-olds drive. To further her argument, she wrote, "It really is an eyesore." I had to ask her, "What's an eyesore?" I won as "Alderman for a Day," but I never understood how the selection committee didn't see through an essay filled with a 43-year-old woman's expression of civil discontent disguised as what should've been a kid's stab at winning the opportunity to participate in a City Council meeting. By "participate" I mean answering, "Here" to roll call and "It's on the 4th of July," when asked, "When will the July 4th fireworks take place?" The other winners were the typical handful of kids born with steel traps for brains and had only each other in their classes since kindergarten. I was never one of those people and nobody found that odd either? For a group photo, I stood next to a Korean girl who played 3 instruments, crushed any sport and burned holes through books with her eyes. Wow. Point out what doesn't belong kids; I may as well have been wearing a shoe on my head. But in terms of writing my Girl College essay, I think Mom's real concern was that I'd choose an embarrassing subject: *Christy McNichol* for her brave performance in *Little Darlings? Wonder Woman* for believing her invisible plane was a better hiding place than a real one? *Betty Boop?* I'm not so sure and I've never been compelled to ask. The important thing is, I took the subsequent acceptance and ran.

I spent one year at Girl College and had no desire to return. Don't get me wrong, the campus was fairly scenic, I got along with my roommates well enough and most of my instructors were interesting to the point where I didn't leave class feeling less intelligent than before I walked in. Every morning, the cafeteria served warm, homemade, still chewy-in-the-center chunks of granola piled in a huge bowl for our taking. Although a huge selling point for the school in my opinion, it was just not enough to keep me there. The biggest issue I had about this place was the all-women's college so-called "dynamic," mostly because there wasn't much of one. At least, not one that was particularly useful if a student eventually decided to assimilate with members of the opposite sex. To pursue a higher education at an all-women's school with plans to live on Earth rather than Venus after graduation, was like playing a game of catch with yourself and later expecting to make the farm team. Honestly, a Protestant summer camp in Utah functioned on a more progressive philosophy. But this was just my gripe; plenty of people were happy there and managed to make it in a normal social-occupational stratum. Each graduating class did not spit out 500, 21-year-old nuns, cloistered 100 yards from campus, doomed to a life of celibacy and baking bland bread to sell at the farmer's market. But as much as I knew this, it still felt pointless for me to be there, I was in collegiate purgatory at best and life's just too short for that.

First, there was no "college town" to speak of. Oh, sure there was the good ol' center of town, but it was about 10 miles away and had zero student attractions. Now, if a girl had an interest in butchery, there was a "Moo 'n Oink" that must have purchased every second of advertising time on local TV. There was no main drag, late night diners and certainly no pseudo-hippie planted in the quad playing acoustic while singing the only 2 verses he knew from "Fire and Rain." There wasn't anywhere to get a job other than the school's cafeteria, no Greek system, no coffee shop and no nightlife. Unless you consider riding a bus filled with headbands and wool blazers to the nearby coed (brother) university, "nightlife." Bus-loads of girls were dumped on their campus hoping some schmuck would invite us to a dorm party, and then of course we, as the bigger schmucks, followed happy as larks.

During the year, I befriended a couple sophomores: fun loving broads who lived in my dorm and conveniently had access to a car. It was a damp, cool October weeknight when they invited me, my roommate, someone's boyfriend and a couple random bored girls into their *Toyota* to check out a "townie" bar with a posses-sive name like "DJ's" or "Bud's." Not only was this place notorious for serving alcohol to minors; it was a well-established watering hole for locals. Reminiscent of *Elmer Fudd's Looney Tunes Lounge,* there was a gigantic bar that resembled a fallen sequoia tree left to petrify for a century, until somebody decided to surround it with walls and use it to serve drinks. There were a couple rows of brown, hackneyed laminate tables and a defunct fireplace hiding in the corner with a sign attached that read, "No children allowed in fireplace." Scattered on the dark, paneled walls were dispropor-tionately small photos of NASCAR has-beens and local newscast-ers from the 1970s in cheap, glassless picture frames. The patrons sure seemed to be enjoying themselves as they chatted with the

80-year-old waitress and didn't bat an eyelash when several minors blasted in for cheap beer and a stab at the jukebox with the illuminated rainbow cascading across the top. Like a noisy gem, the bulky box sat smack in the middle of the room as it interrupted a filthy, decades-old trail of carpet that was forged by work boots trudging their way to the bathroom. Unsure of how our evening was going to go down, I took a seat and stared at the rainbow lights for a few minutes before pitchers of Only God Knows What Light were placed before us. We swilled several cups of the off white liquid that we called "beer" and were very loudly getting to know each other at an exponential rate, but didn't bother to catch each other's names. It's interesting how two barely-there acquaintances can quickly learn intimate details about each other due to a couple weak commonalities: 1. We go to the same school. 2. Intoxication deteriorated our social filters:

Drunk 1: "Oh my God, I totally had to squat when I used the bathroom, gross."

Drunk 2: "Oh my God I knooow! Like, do people just pee on the seat?"

Drunk 1: "My cousin does that but she's mental."

Drunk 2: "Oh my God, at the EtaPi house somewhere, totally had to go in the woods, like helloooo roofees?"

Drunk 1: "Who's Rufus?"

Drunk 2: "I know right?"

There was significant bonding taking place here. As if trading our war-stories wasn't obnoxious enough, we had to (very loudly) sing the <u>one</u> verse from Billy Joel's "Captain Jack" that we all knew well enough:

"Captain Jack will get you high tonight
And take you to his special island
Captain Jack will get you (mumble - unsure if it's "by" or "high" again)
Just a little push and you'll be SMILINN'"

Stumbling through the rest of the song didn't prevent us from making complete asses of ourselves, no it didn't.

"So you stand on the corner (??pause) ENGLAND clothes
And you look so good uh, (?) right down to ...(?????) TOES
uhh
but you're (pause) still (pause) PICK YOUR NOSE,"

I'm not sure if Billy Joel's *Piano Man* was the only CD housed in that jukebox, or if the self-appointed jukebox "manager" (the person who brought enough cash to fend for herself and not rely on strange, old farmers to foot our bar tab), designated "Captain Jack" as our theme song. It didn't matter that it's about ungrateful suburban lost souls who narcissistically flush their lives down the toilet every time they score some Acapulco Gold. It was our anthem for a couple of hours, plus musically, it's a fantastic song. We left the bar happily singing and stupid and I finally felt like I wasn't breaking curfew at Bible camp. The seven of us piled into the *Toyota* and began our trek back to campus. It was a long, 10-minute ride in blinding darkness except for the incandescent glare from our own headlights. There was no reciprocal light from oncoming cars, which would have at least reassured me that we were on route to civilization and not driving in a crop circle. Sitting on the lap of Drunk 1, I was just about to fall asleep when a huge, semicircle of light caught my eye. Realizing the glow was the entrance to campus, I was relieved to be out of Dukes of Hazzardville's public house, minutes from my bed and many hours from my next class.

Not 30 seconds after mentally preparing to say goodnight to my new nameless friends, I saw the reflection of flashing police lights on the back of the driver's headrest. Anyone who has ever been tailed by a police car goes through a few moments of denial when she tells herself, "He's probably after that spray-painted *El Camino* that just sped past me at 80 mph with its muffler scraping the pavement. Am I in the way? I'll pull-over so he can get through." (Why not increase stress by negotiating with yourself as a lame attempt to make the truth less true?) I broke the silence and uttered, "Why are their lights still on?" as if their initial purpose was obviously to entertain the imaginary children standing on the side of the road in the dark. No one responded to my query, maybe because it was stupid and we were obviously being pursued. Was our driver speeding? Was the taillight broken with a hand sticking out of it? No *El Camino* blew by us, but our trusty driver spent a good 3 minutes of police crawl before she finally surrendered at the edge of campus. She rolled her window down as the policeman approached the car, "Do you know it's illegal to have this many people in a car?" he said. I assumed we were going to be told go home. "Everybody out of the vehicle," he commanded. We spilled out of the car as directed and stood in a line so the officer could shine his flashlight in our faces. "Has anyone been drinking tonight?" he asked. (Someone needs to think of a new line for situations like this.) Nobody had to walk on a chalk line while she counted backwards and touch her nose to determine intoxication; the cop went right for the Breathalyzer apparatus. One-by-one we blew into this contraption and waited for a response. ".097...that's past the legal limit. I'll need your ID," he said to the first blower. ".135, .065, .174," he announced while his quiet, skinny rookie partner collected IDs and wrote tickets. As I waited for *my* score, I slightly turned my head and saw my brightly lit, ugly, brown dorm across the field - so close and yet, so far away. Finally it was my turn. "Blow into this mouthpiece until instructed further." I did just that. ".18!! She has a .18!!" he snarled, "That's **waaay** over the limit!" Evidently, a minor blowing .18 on a Breathalyzer is more illegal than a minor blowing a .175. He cockily sauntered to the opposite side of the car, turned away from me and began to speak with his partner. "You should bolt," my inner voice told me, "now or never." This is not the same voice that tried to convince myself moments earlier that the fuzz was really after a phantom *El Camino*. This voice comes from a place of such great depth, it typically pipes-up in life compromising circumstances such as, running from prehistoric wildlife or a parachute malfunction over the Dead Sea riddled with pirates. It's a voice you must listen to, even if you think it's trying to ruin you at the time. I caught my roommate's eye to inform her of my plan: I made a slashing gesture across my throat, exaggeratedly mouthed, "I'm going," while I pointed my thumb behind me toward our dorm. (A pantomime I've never lived down.) "RUN!! NOW!!" said the voice. So I did.

I ran like I was fleeing the Bolshevik Revolution. I ran like I discovered an open window in the juvenile corrections center's cafeteria.

I literally ran like my life depended on it because if I got arrested, my parents would've stuffed me in a box and shipped it to a work camp. Or worse, saw to it that I work the rest of my life in a cubicle. A beige cubicle. I zeroed-in on my dorm bouncing up and down in the distance with my every step, occasionally blurring when un-leveled ground threw a blip in my gait. The cold air made my throat feel like I gargled liquid nitrogen so I focused on a street lamps' amorphous beam as a distraction. It's not like I could have stopped to take a breather behind a tree, an open field is not exactly an inconspicuous escape route. When the oversized, zip-up-to-form-a-scarf collar on my big, red *Land's End* Jacket began to whip me in the face was when I saw this escapade transcend from badass to downright ludicrous.

Occasionally in horror movies, there will be a scene when a mother and child are crouched in a tiny space attempting to hide from impending doom. Frightened out of their minds, the mother tries to calm her daughter by rocking her like a baby, while singing her favorite childhood song. Essentially that's what I was doing for myself, only in monotone. After all, I was running and who was going to rock me?

"CaptinJackwillgetyouhightonightandtakeyoutohisspecialislandCaptain Jackwillgetyoubytonightjustanotherhitandyou'llbesmilingwatermenolbal blahNewEnglandclooooothes..."

When I finally made it to the dorm and yanked open the door, I looked to my right and noticed a campus security car drive by. Again I was hoping for that *El Camino*. I stumbled over the thresh-old and rather than beeline to my room, I, for reasons I've yet to understand, hid in the single-stalled public bathroom located about 10 feet from the entrance. I locked myself in the stall and stood there silently for about 60 seconds before I heard a woman's muffled voice from outside the bathroom. Not a 19-year-old's voice, but a 50-something, *Chesterfield*-smoking, campus security voice. "What do I do what do I do what do I do?" I thought while spinning around the stall as if this was going to contain my fleeting thoughts. I felt like a cat in a shower.

I looked up and saw a vent, not a particularly large vent, just your average vent. Still affected by coursing endorphins and whatnot, delusions of grandeur set in. This was 1991 and the television show *MacGyver* was hugely popular and in its 6th season. Everybody loved *MacGyver*; he was a renegade with a mullet who could single-handedly save the world from a plummeting meteor by using only a tampon and some correction fluid. Save a little girl from kidnappers? He'd create SONAR from her hairbrush and the wind hitting a cooking funnel. *MacGyver* rocked and so did I. Or at least that's what my clouded brain thought at the time.

I can honestly say that I looked at that vent and thought, "I wonder if I can fit through there and crawl through the duct system to escape whoever is out there...like...like *MacGyver*." Even my thoughts were slurred. It didn't occur to me that I did not have a ladder and a drill handy to remove the vent cover in the first place. I continued to reason, "But what if I get stuck, form a human clog and cause the whole building to blow-up?" Yes, really. Eventually, I realized that my shoes were the only things that could have easily fit through that vent and given my alcoholic impairment, probably saw that as only a minor setback. My engineering fantasies were quickly thwarted when I heard the bathroom door open, followed by slow and steady foot-steps, then a pause. "Hello?" said the visitor. It was Campus Officer Lady Chesterfield. I could see her beige uniform and sensible shoes through the crack in the stall.

"Something. Something. There must be something," I thought, I could hear my heart pounding. "Come out of the stall please," said Chesterfield. "County is looking for you." (I'd indicate swear words here, but this is a family book.) The vent idea blew out the window and I was completely trapped and there was no option for me other than to exit the stall. Knowing she must have had a description of me; long brown hair, red jacket with giant, floppy collar, running like a lunatic through a field, I looked at my springy, coiled keychain wrapped around my wrist, similar to what retail employees wear to unlock dressing rooms. My inner (special) *MacGyver* kicked-in again when I haphazardly gathered my hair on the top of my head and used my coiled keychain, with the keys still attached, as a ponytail holder. To further my impulsive brilliance, I turned my red jacket inside out so the navy blue lining was on the outside and proceeded to put it on. There I stood, my cheeks stained with old mascara, hair intertwined with my keychain, wearing my inside out jacket with its frayed seams exposed. "There," I thought. She'll never know it's me."

"Come out of the stall please," said Chesterfield. As I stood there convinced I was masterfully disguised, I took a deep breath and told myself to act naturally. I flushed the toilet like I was in the stall for a legit reason, unlocked the door and sauntered out. I glanced at Chesterfield with bloodshot eyes and an expression I hoped con-veyed, "Oh... hi, fancy meeting you here. Excuse me, I just need to get to the sink to wa…" "You know there is a description of you," said Officer Lady Chesterfield. "All of county police's alerts come to us." I looked at her blankly with my keys still dangling against my head. It was time to accept the end of my stint at large. She backed-up toward the bathroom exit and positioned her body as a human blockade. Looking down to her right, she began to fidget with the deadbolt lock and faceplate located on the inside of the doorframe. "You see this?" she said. I said nothing. She pointed to the lock and said, "This only works," then to the matching faceplate, "if it fits into this." I had no idea where she was going with this. For all I know she could've said, "You only get a spork if your spoon is amiss," or "The lemur lurks, in the cold abyss," or "You know you're a dork if you make many lists." Nothing was making sense at this moment except when she looked at me and said, "Go upstairs and go to bed." So I thanked her genuinely but quickly so she didn't have time to change her mind and ran up to my room.

Nothing came of those tickets given to the remaining 6 kids who I left on the outskirts of campus. But that was it for me, it was time to find another school. It's not that I was a particularly troubled person who was just waiting to be unleashed to the world. I just needed to be a part of whatever sliver of "reality" I could get. I had no plans to jump on the next plane to Berkeley or NYU, but having males in my class was a good start. Mom wanted me to stay another year, but got tired of listening to me on the phone every day threaten to go to a beauty school advertised in the back of *MAD Magazine*. But for the short time at Girl College, thank you Mom, Barbara Bush and without a doubt, Officer Lady Chesterfield.

---

* "Illegal Alien" by Genesis, 1983

CHAPTER 2

*Houses of the Holy

Whether from everyday life or multimedia, we continuously gather sociocultural information to store in our mental file folders. But with limited exposure to cultures unlike our own, it's easy to stuff our "not me" files with stick-figure depictions until a *Quick Look* into their world is needed. Although a common and natural occurrence, it is the premise to something I call "Self-Deprecating Discrimination" **(SDD)**. Stick with me here. This is not the good old-fashioned discrimination we're familiar with, the kind that causes riots, homicides and disturbing chapters in history books. **SDD** is positive stereotyping to compensate for your ineptitude about other cultures. After all, admitting harmless ignorance is better than being misconstrued as offensive. We've all been guilty, it happens to the best of us, so here's an example:

White person: "Excuse me please...hi, may I have EL FORKO GRACIAS? It's 'gracias' right? Ok just wanted it to be right.... great thanks. I mean GRACIAS."

White person hopes to convey: "I'm speaking sorry-ass Spanish, because I don't want you to think I'm a patronizing Caucasian. I know there is more to your culture than working in restaurants, but this is the only place we've interacted. So, asking you for a fork while butchering your language is how I'm showing appreciation for your killer work ethic. I'm sorry for dropping my first fork with the hunk of cheesecake still attached and I hope you can read my mind."

Let's breakdown the **SDD** process further:

One
Gather cultural information: All the Asian kids in school spend half the day in the gifted class and can play "Flight of the Bumblebee" on any given wind instrument. I had a Chinese friend once, he was afraid his mother would hurt him if he played my video games, so he played chess with Dad.

Stick-figure drawing: Asians are born geniuses and fear their parents. I've never encountered a stupid or loud Asian so, there's no way the average white boy can keep up with one in business, discipline or spatial relations.

SDD in action: "Don't give me the bill to split 5 ways, give it to Pfung. He'll do it in his head, if he hadn't already while we were ordering."

Two
Gather cultural information: The Gay men in my yoga class are unbelievably attractive, stylish, have six packs and no body hair. They're funny, never depressed, love clubbing and styling women's

hair. On sitcoms, they rock an open-concept kitchen/living room without it ever looking like it's been pillaged by jackals.

Stick-figure drawing: Gay men are the perpetually hot, stylish, fun and tidy people women can't marry. Befriending a gay man would be awesome because he'd *always* hang out with me and if I were single, father my awesome baby.

SDD in action: "You're gay right? Will you braid my hair? Do you like my house? If you tell me I'm pretty, I may as well be perfect and therefore emotionally prepared to die."

Three
At one time, my ideas of Jewish people suffered from SDD in a big way:

Gather cultural information: Mom used to say that in her next life, she is going to be a Jewish doctor's wife and live on Chicago's North Shore; Barbara Streisand, Albert Einstein and many physicians are Jewish; they don't do Christmas but get presents for 8 days instead. Jealous, I want eight laptops! They believe Jesus was a prophet and a "great man." (It's funny how they politely explain their Jesus to us Gentiles. "Oh yes we believe he existed, but as a person and not as God's imaginary kid. Sorry."); Hebrew must be a dead language because I've only seen it on top of Crucifixes; according to news footage, nobody goes to Israel without packing an AK 47 and staying in a cave under the sand.

Stick-figure drawing: Jewish people are smart, wealthy, entertaining and not plumbers. We all know they invented bagels.

Jewish boyfriends pay for everything and love their mothers. The folk wearing the funky hats and long, sideburn curls, I've learned are not Amish.

SDD in action: My first health insurance plan after college, provided a list of physicians for my use. Other than location, I chose doctors with names I liked: Katz, Silver, Gold, Fine, Sweet or compounded versions. Thorough huh? My last name was long and Croatian and these names were succinct, easy to spell, pleasant sounding and yes, Jewish. So maybe I was inadvertently wooing Jewish doctors. It must have been foreshadowing though, I did end up marrying a nice Jewish boy. Except he's not a doctor and he doesn't have one of these cute, precious metal names.

To the best of my knowledge, I had never met a Jewish person until my sophomore year of college. That's 19 years withheld from the chosen people and still, I had a considerable head start on many of my childhood peers. I transferred out of Girl College to State University where less than 10% of the student body was Jewish. Even their nationally recognized Jewish fraternity only had "token Jews." Despite the apparent shortage, the homogeneous student population didn't seem odd to me, simply because it was consistent with what I already knew and comparable to watching *Riverdance* through a paper towel tube.

My first introduction to "the tribe" was my little roommate who was a Rhode Island transfer. She was a tiny girl with olive skin, brown eyes, dark, brown hair and maintained a perfect, pink, squared-tipped manicure. She wore real clothes like skirts, tights and blazers to her morning classes, spent the holidays with her puppy "Champagne" and grandparents in Boca Raton. She pronounced my name "Shah-rin" and I thought she was Hawaiian or maybe even Greek. So did my mom. It didn't take long for her to say to me with disbelief, "No you dumbass, I'm Jewish." Immediately my brain recalled, "Oooh right.... No Christmas person." Having deviated from Yom Kippur fasts with lobster and Prosecco, I was not surprised when I caught all 4'10" of her standing on a ridiculously tall ladder hanging Christmas lights in our apartment. I laughed and she responded, "F--k off! I've always wanted to do this."

Despite searching for a "nice Jewish boy" to marry, she dated many a "Goy" (see glossary at the end of chapter), including an obsessed 6'4"WASPy guy who'd buy her jewelry after she'd tell him to "shut the f--k up!" She strung-along one poor dolt until after graduation because she wanted to "hold-out for a house." It didn't happen. I found myself dating a couple of her claimed future husbands, one of whom explained to me, "Oh No! Mom drives the *Mercedes* and Dad drives the practical car." I was stymied. I thought he was joking. When I was a child, Mom drove the practical car and Dad drove the nicer car, a common arrangement for most folks in my community. "Shah-rin!!" quipped my little roommate, "G-d damn it! You take all the good Jews!!" During parents' weekend, she couldn't wait to introduce my then-boyfriend to her mother. "My mother is going to plotz, (again, see the glossary), when she meets him!" She wasn't too interested in introducing him as "Shah-rin's boyfriend," as much as "Mom, shouldn't he be my husband? Isn't he perfect?"

There is something to be said for the "nice Jewish boy" ideology, but first, I must explain the "The Jewish Mother." From birth, she teaches her son (via verbal persistence, guilt and/or beating with soup ladle) to revere his mother, his friends' mothers and any other important female in his life. This may include every female in his extended

family and any woman the mother has taken a liking to and hence-
forth claimed as either your "cousin" or "aunt." It could be the greeter
at *Walmart,* but if they're tight and she's Jewish (not likely, but I'm
using *WalMart* for emphasis), she's your cousin or aunt. It's important
to understand that *all* mothers have the *potential to be* Jewish Mothers
and tell her kid 10 times to bring a jacket; insist that her adult child
is "going to be late" for the job she's had for several years; provoke
guilt by saying, "That's all you're going to eat? Your blood sugar will
drop and you'll collapse on your way home from class. There could
be a snow storm, no one will be able to find you and THEN… there'd
be nothing left for ME to do but kill myself, *just* so I could be with
you." However, due to cultural differences, not all mothers express
this potential. The Jewish mother made a name for herself because
she shares her thoughts when she sees fit (always) and with heightened frequency (loudly). Case in point: my 100% Irish, other side of
the world, non-culturally Jewish mother does not automatically pipe
into my business as soon as she's concerned. Her way is to stay out,
and silently ruminate until her stress level rises to a critical mass so
powerful, her inner "Jewish Mother" tips over and spills right onto
someone's conscience. Literally minutes before my now-husband
rang the doorbell for our 3rd or 4th date, she hit me with, "Are you
comfortable with renouncing Jesus Christ?" or my favorite, "If you
die, will you still be able to have a Catholic funeral?" (Her tears here.)

The more life we live, the fuller our filing cabinets become. Currently,
my cabinet contains an accordion folder that runneth over with a nice
Jewish boy, aka "Husband," who's obsessed with golf and unfortunately, RUN DMC. (It's painful watching him try to be black. I mean,
it hurts my head). We've been married for 15 years and I can attest to
the results of Jewish mothering, because Husband understands that
outsourcing is a necessary expense. Bubbie, his mother, always says,

"The mother makes the mood of the house, so why suffer?" For instance, hiring a babysitter (who I encourage my children to also call "Mommy") happy to monitor your kid during that hour-long "Music and Movement" class preserves your sanity and ultimately everybody else's. Similarly, so does ordering (quality) food for Thanksgiving dinner should it become imperative for any reason. I've experienced too many Thanksgivings when Mom was overworked and under-appreciated. Ever find yourself anxiety ridden over a broken crystal goblet? Cooking all day when you hate to feed people? Sell the crystal, order good food and have a drink. You won't see me flogging myself later out of guilt.

I now live in a modern day suburban little Israel and my immersion has been both fascinating and awakening. I've never felt the need to convert or memorize anything from a soft-covered textbook with a picture of Hasidic Jews lighting candles on the cover. What would be the point? It's more the culture than the religion that's made 30 miles away feel like a foreign land. Plus religious fundamentals won't explain what "schvitz" means. There have been many conversations when seemingly out of nowhere I was tossed a guttural Yiddish word that the pitcher assumed I understood:

Cousin Pearl: "My little <u>mutchkie</u> mamma you must visit me in Arizona. It's a <u>schlepp,</u> but the ladies in my Mahjong group will just <u>kvell</u> over you hghony," (guttural "honey").

Sharon: "I'm sorry, but what does "ka vell" mean? Did you say something about a "munchkin?"

Was Cousin Pearl confused? Was this a side effect from the stroke? Is she really related?

Ah, the Yiddish. The historical language of Ashkenazi Jews references back to the 12th century and has budded in different forms depending on history and geography. Modern Eastern Yiddish, the kind your gynecologist uses when he says, "Scoot your tushie to the end of the table," is a blend of Hebrew, Slavic, Polish, Eastern Hungarian, Ukrainian, Galician, Lithuanian, Belarusian and a touch of romance languages tightly wrapped in a Germanic-based vernacular. Unless your great Bubbie and Zadie are visiting from the old country for 6 months, the people of Jewish Chicago typically don't walk around speaking their motherland's Yiddish or even remotely know it in its entirety. Select Yiddish words and phrases are used about as frequently as the words "vacuum," "milk" or "clean this up." They don't occupy a lot of space in the Jewish Chicago lexicon but their decoding is integral to understanding what the hell somebody is talking about.

There is no end to the Yiddish words and expressions used regularly so it was necessary for me to learn, at the very least, the following words in order to effectively communicate with neighbors, visiting distant "cousins" and owners of small boutiques with negotiable pricing:

1. **Bisl (noun):** A little bit.
   "Why don't you have a *bisl* of brisket before bed hghoney? It'll settle your stomach."

2. **Boychik (noun):** A term of endearment for a beloved son. Also known as "The Golden Son."
   "My *boychik*...look at him in his Bar Mitzvah suit and Tallit. Uhx, (guttural "Uh"), Gawd. Didn't I tell you he's gifted?"

3. **Bubbie (noun):** Grandmother. Any spelling is acceptable because according to your *Buby*, you can do no wrong. Typically characterized by a love to feed her people and buy them new wardrobes.
   "*Bubbe* said I deserve only the best of the best and to not worry about the money."

4. **Elijah (noun):** A prophet or wonder worker "invited" to religious holidays as indicated by an open door and an empty chair at the dinner table.
   "Unkie, *Elijah's* chair is only empty because Grandpa shuffled-off to take a nap, so you can stop knocking on the table now. The door's open anyway."

5. **Feh! (expression):** To indicate disgust representative of spitting. How the sound "feh" came from spitting is not fully understood.
   "*Feh!* Mayonnaise on white bread? With what? Ham? *Feh!*"

6. **From Hunger (Anglicized expression):** Of poor quality.
   "Oy! The fabric on this sofa is *from hunger* and should be burned already!"

7. **Futz (noun, verb):** To waste time frivolously or by unnecessary trial and error. Form of "arum fartzen" literally meaning, "to fart about."
   Noun: "Such a dumb *futz* that plumber was for telling me chicken bones sharpen the disposal blades. His head should have been on the platter, not the chicken's."

Verb: "Melvin, if you keep *futzing*-around with your medications, you'll go blind again and be useless."

8. **Gefilte Fish (noun):** English translation - "stuffed fish." I like to refer to it as the Jewish hotdog due to its questionable combination of ground, deboned whitefish or carp and is often eaten as an appetizer. In other words, it's what Jewish people from Eastern Europe ate when there was nothing else available. Being very *Fiddler on the Roof*, people today claim to love it in the name of "tradition." I don't buy it.
"Catherine honey, what's wrong? You don't like *gefilte fish*? Cousin Rachel slaved for *hours* over Bubbie's 19th century meat grinder to make it just for you! You know what? It's ok …… Milton! Don't pressure her!!"
Honey, if you don't want it, just throw it out. The staple of our people."

9. **Gottenyu (expression):** A substitute for "oh God," to express despair, anguish or pity for something.
"We spent $300,000 to send you to this fabulous university and you want to flush it all away to become a plumber? Oy *Gottenyu*! Marvin my blood pressure is escalating. Call your cousin."

10. **Goy (noun, adjective):** A non-Jew or Gentile. Although the origin of its meaning is not derogatory, Americanized-Jewish slang associates "Goy" with bland food or anything bland for that matter. The average Goy has no idea what a "Goy" is anyway and those who do, don't care.
Noun: *Goy* moved in next door? Milton, the neighborhood is changing. Quick! Cover the pool!"

Adjective: "I should have known better than to go to that *Goy* bakery for a cinnamon swirl loaf, it looks like a brown and white sponge for Pete's sake."

11. **Hazer (noun):** A greedy person or one who eats like a pig. "That *hazer* wanted more brisket for himself and that's why he cut it along the grain I tell you."

12. **Kenahora pu, pu, pu (expression):** Kenahora loosely means to keep the "evil eye" away and "pu, pu, pu" indicates spitting on the demon. Used together as a colloquialism to superstitiously avoid bad luck or jinxing a positive occurrence. To me, that's a lot of syllables, so I'd rather knock on wood.
"My grandchildren are being raised Jewish and have no idea they're really Catholic. *Kenahora poo, poo, poo.*"

13. **Kibitz (verb):** To chat informally or to meddle and give unwanted advice.
"It's your grand-cousin's Shiva and you think it's a *kibitz* fest? What's wrong with you?"

14. **Kvell (verb):** To be proud, overjoyed and overwhelmed with delight.
"Why can't I *kvell* over you Rabbi? My daughter, she's single you know...and gifted."

15. **Kvetch (noun, verb):** To complain or whine. The k and v are pronounced together like "kfetch" without too much emphasis on k, v or f sounds. Expect to be corrected after attempting to pronounce it.

Noun: "What a *kvetch* that woman is insisting on a *Viking* stove during the inspection. Who does she think she is, Streisand?"
Verb: "There are CHILDREN starving in China and you're *kvetching* about your chunky highlights? Enough already Leah!"

16. **Mensch (noun or adjective):** A good, honest, trustworthy person or one to emulate.
Noun: "What a *mensch* you are for shoveling your great grand-cousin Pearl's walkway so she doesn't kill herself. Imagine if you didn't."
Adjective: "Zachary, it's not very *menschy* when you hide from Mommy under the mannequin's skiiirt."

17. **Mishegas (noun):** Insanity or craziness.
"Not to worry honey, we all have our own *mishegas*. So what's wrong with you now?"

18. **Nudnik (noun):** An annoying, pestering and/or boring person, or anyone who bothers you for any reason.
"I had to play 18 holes with this *nudnik* today. All he talked about was his outdoor, pizza oven and then I caught him futzing with the scorecard. The nerve."

19. **Oy (exclamation):** Short for "Oy vey," "Oy vey iz mir" or "Woe is me." An expression used to express minor, past, present or impending tragedy.
"*Oy*! As soon as I sit to watch *Guiding Light*, something happens to the DVR."

20. **Patchke (verb):** To mess around with.
    "That's enough *patchke*-ing with the mayonnaise already! You're going to get food poisoning!"

21. **Polkies (noun):** Beefy thighs (preferably on a baby) that any proud Bubbie wants "to chew on."
    "Oy Gott ("Gott," the ghetto version of "God" cancels the negative "oy"), those *polkies*. I can't stand it! I just want to put them in a bun and chew on them! His pants are too small. What's wrong with you?!"

22. **Schlepp (noun, verb, adjective):** To carry something awkward or heavy for a long journey.
    Noun: "Oy vey. What a *schlepp* it was from the deli with that whitefish tray."
    Adjective: "Feh! Your suit looks *schleppy* without the gold tie I bought for you."
    Derogatory Noun: "He dropped out of med school to run off with your aesthetician? What a *schlepp*."
    Verb: "Enough *schlepping* of this salami already."

not to be confused with

23. **Schmaltz (noun, adjective):** Melted fat or a reference to anything greasy that produces ample fat drippings. Also used to describe something overly sentimental.
    Noun: "You mean you'd dip your bread into that *schmaltz* and eat it? Are you looking for a coronary?"
    Adjective: "Oy what a *schmaltzy* musical that *Cats* was. What is everybody so upset about? They're Cats for G-d's sake! Your father. He hates cats."

not to be confused with

24. **Schmear (noun, verb):** Commonly refers to a thick condiment one spreads on a bagel.
Noun: "Milton! Be a mensch and put a *schmear* of lox spread on half a poppy seed (bagel) would ya'?"
Verb: "Oy! I know your tendinitis is acting up from working 18-hour shifts for your brain surgery rotation. Can I *schmear* some *Temptee* on a bialy and feed it to you, my handsome boychik?"

not to be confused with

25. **Schmutz (noun, adjective):** A substance of unpleasant appearance and texture found in an undesirable place, typically on one's person or an inanimate object.
Noun: "Ugh, there's *schmutz* hanging from Uncle Abe's mustache again."
Verb: "You think I'm going to hold on to that subway pole after that homeless man got it all *schmutzy?*"

not to be confused with

26. **Schvitz (verb, adjective):** Profuse sweating.
Verb: "*DisneyWorld* in June? Are you kidding? The *schvitzing* is enough to put you in a mental institution."
Adjective: "Will getting all *schvitzy* during Bikram yoga screw-up my Keratin treatment?"

27. **Shayna Punim (noun):** A pretty face often shortened to "punim" when used as a direct compliment.

"What a *shayna punim* on that baby. Did you see? Isn't it about time you had one?"

28. **Shmy (noun, verb):** To shop around or leisurely window-shop.
Noun: "What were you expecting Lori, the world on a string? This walk down Madison Avenue was just a *shmy*!"
Verb: "Robyn, honey, your frequent *shmying* has made you the most recognized person in the retail district. You should be proud honey."

not to be confused with

29. **Shpilkes (noun):** A state of agitation or impatience.
"Your cousin had *shpilkes* during the entire service. He must be on drugs."

30. **Tottie (noun):** A term of endearment for a little boy. This also, can be spelled any way you choose.
"Look at my *Tottie* pretending to use my charge plate. I just want to EAT HIM UP!!"

31. **Tuchus (noun):** Buttocks.
"You better lay off the babka or you'll wake up with a double *tuchus*!"

32. **Tumult (noun):** A riot or uprising. Noise made by a crowd.
"Oy the *tumult* the triplets made with their deadly plague finger puppets. Adorable but enough already, your father's hungry."

33. **Zadie (noun):** Bubby's husband. Any spelling is acceptable because Bube won't have you corrected. Typically characterized by leading the Seder, listening to Bubbe, looking through the obituaries and saying, "Let's see if I made it through the night." He's on the quiet side, intelligent, pays for a lot of things and plays a lot of golf. If Bubbe's little grand-baby prince agitates Zadi enough, he may yell at him if Bubbi isn't around.

"*Zayde! Zadey!* Tell us about the time you killed a man to escape the Communists! Oh! Then can you show us the foot with the missing toe again? Please??"

Over the past 13 years, I've accumulated enough Yiddish in my arsenal to impress the elders, confuse my parents and entertain my peers. Philanthropically, I've used it to educate non-Jews who live as the minority in our community and need cocktail party fodder for their law firm's Holiday bash or to impress the partner's wife when promotions are in the forecast. I also translate for the non-Jewish mothers during bake sales and sleepover drop-offs. When I see that quizzical look, I'll quickly intercede with a hand on her shoulder and the discreet, encouraging words, "Dear child, I've been where you are. Let me help you, help me, to help you again. Just make sure everyone is fed first."

---

* "Houses of the Holy" by Led Zeppelin, 1973

CHAPTER 3

*Obvious Child

Husband's parents are Floridians so we told them about their first grand-fetus over the phone. Back in 2002, only blue-chip CEOs owned $500, golf ball-sized computer cameras. Even if we owned one, the image quality made everybody look like fractals so we had to imagine Bubbie's visceral reaction. I didn't need a camera to know that she was wringing her manicured hands, shifting from foot to foot and could barely contain herself from jump-starting "Tottie's" *Neiman Marcus* gift registry. Any subsequent hypertension quickly resolved once she sat down to register online. "My son!" she said, followed by a pause. A speechless Bubbie is a rare occurrence that can only indicate extreme happiness, confusion or anger. We weren't married long enough to provoke the latter, so happy or confused she was.

About 3 months into the pregnancy, Husband and I flew to Orlando to stay in his childhood home for over a week and yes, Orlando actually does have residents. As we walked outside into the "arrival pick-up" area, the heavy, balmy air hit me like a hot air balloon deflated in my face; quite the contrast to Chicago's icy stalagmite wind puncturing your body. (FYI, it stabs your soul as well, so after living through a couple of winters, your spirit deadens just enough for you to carry on.) Through a dirty, hot layer of wavy airport air, we saw Bubbie and Zadie standing outside their SUV while talking on their cell phones. They waved all 4 arms to get our attention, like they were lost in the Bermuda Triangle, even though we were only about 20 feet away. As we approached their car, I heard blaring from Bubbie's phone, "HAS THE EAGLE LANDED??!!" I guess Sharon with fetus equaled the first manned, lunar mission. Fine, I'll take it.

Our stay with Bubbie and Zadie was a week filled with aunts, uncles, cousins (either biological or acquired), and family friends visiting to see Husband and ask me, "Where's the baby?" Apparently 3 months into my first pregnancy, I was expected to look like I was carrying a pack of bison. I'm not sure if the missing baby comments concerned her, but Bubbie had an unbreakable plan to take me shopping for maternity clothes and ignored my efforts to decline her very generous but premature offer. Maybe she thought that wearing maternity clothes would have made me look pregnant enough to keep the relatives happy. I explained that I was many weeks away from looking pregnant (rather than just overfed) and actually "needing" maternity clothes. Meanwhile, I planned to wear my regular clothes modified with larger frumpy shirts and rubber bands to extend the waist area where the button would normally meet its hole. It's not as bad as swimsuit shopping, but diving into the abyss of overpriced and generally dislikable pregnant person clothes was something I chose to avoid until absolutely necessary. "What's the difference? I'm not taking my money with me when I die, so let me buy you what I want! If you end-up hating them, throw them out. What do I care?" It was tricky getting my point across to a person who was generous to a fault and loved to spend for sport. The last time I attempted to stop her from buying me an embarrassing amount of clothing, she yelled at me in *Ann Taylor*. "Don't do that, don't...DO...that!" she said pointing her bejeweled scolding finger at me as we stood at the register. So off we went to the maternity boutique - Mrs. Surly and Mrs. Overzealous. Together we balanced out, couldn't we just have called it a day?

I knew I was coming home with at least $150 worth of useful t-shirts and a pair of jeans along with about $500 worth of completely impractical clothing. She kept tossing more and more clothes over the dressing room door that looked absolutely adorable on the store's 14-year-old non-pregnant catalogue model. "Try this!! Try this!!!! Now try this!!!!" A fitted checkered wrap dress; jeans tight everywhere except in the hollow fabric orb where the baby was supposed to be; tent-like tunics and plenty of tight graphic tees that would be pushing it on a kindergartener:

Sharon turns 360 degrees: "Why would I wear this? It's a tube-top with sleeves."

Bubbie: "Oh spare me. That's the faashion! That's what all the pregnant people are wearing!!"

Sharon: "You know hoards of pregnant people?"

Bubbie: "You know, Meryl's cousin? You know, what's-her-name? The woman! The woman uh... (snapping fingers) who owns the sour cream company?"

Sharon: "Um no…"

Bubbie: "Her daughter wears all those shirts that show the belly! That's what everybody does."

Sharon: "Is this alleged sour cream heiress a teenager with a wicked tan?"

Bubbie: "Oy! You know you are just so…you are so…negative! You're going to hurt the baby! You're going to give it a complex! Aunt Ellen already thinks you're going to starve the baby!"

Sharon: "Who's Aunt Ellen?"

I tried-on a fuzzy, pink V-neck cable knit sweater that hung to my knees. It would've made a cute throw draped at the foot of a tween's bed or rocked on a WNBA player, but on me? "Wine cozy" was the first thing that came to mind. And I don't think I've ever used that word before.

Bubbie: "You'll grow into it eventually."

Sharon: "Seriously? This get-up doesn't scream decorative beverage holder to you?"

Bubbie: "The what?........You can wear it with tights! Like a tunic!"

Sharon: "What's a tunic? It just looks like I forgot my pants and all my other clothes for that matter."

Bubbie: "Like a tunic! You know, a tunic!"

Sharon: "More like a wine cozy. You know, for a magnum."

Bubbie: "Huh? Just get it. So you'll have it. You'll take it back if you don't like it. What's the difference?"

I needed the foresight of a Jedi to actually see myself happily "growing into" some of these garments. I could hardly imagine myself waking-up on any given pregnant morning and going right for that thin, clingy, yellowish ecru "maternity" mini-dress and there was no convincing me otherwise. Meanwhile, Bubbie loved taking memorable pictures to eventually lose in a cyber-vacuum and this outing was no exception. She began to dig through her purse for her red gadget camera. She finally found it. However, I've seen this process lead to the misplacement of other important items like: keys, credit cards, phones and other cameras. So I suggested she wear it around her neck like a large pendant:

Bubbie sarcastically: "Cute."

Bubbie: "Now let me take a picture of you to send to Nana in Arizona."

Sharon: "No chance."

I quickly closed the dressing room door. I didn't care who I hurt.

Bubbie: "So can I be in the delivery room?"

Sharon: "I wouldn't let you into the dressing room at *Saks*. What makes you think I will let you in the delivery room?"

Bubbie distracted and ready to move on: "What?.... Ok let's go. What are we buying? Maybe you should get a manicure.

Uhhhh...forget about it. We have to get home to get Zadie dinner or he'll have a hemorrhage."

The hemorrhage expression is a favorite of hers. She had no problem equating internal bleeding with the hunger pangs of a well-fed man.

There was a limit to how much I could argue with her about what she was going to buy for me, so I left the store with enough inappropriately cropped, tight numbers to make her happy. I did eventually return them, as wasting people's hard-earned money is not how I roll. Either the returns didn't bother her or she didn't check her credit card statement because she never asked me, "Why don't you wear that strapless, tie-dye cat suit I got you?"

Well into my 3rd trimester, she became even more hell-bent on showcasing her unborn grandson in any way possible. Even if it superseded common sense, there was no peg too square or hole too round for her to jam together:

Bubbie: "You know, the two of you need to go with us to Arizona to see Nana. She's going to be 90 and you don't want her to die without seeing the baby."

Nana is now 100 years old.

Sharon: "No."

Bubbie: "What do you mean *no?*"

Sharon: "Well, the baby won't be born by then."

Bubbie: "You need to see her! Besides...I'm the mother. You have to do what I say."

Sharon: "You're not the mother anymore."

Bubbie: "We'll get a you a wheelchair so you won't have to walk through the airport."

Sharon: "You know I'll still be 36 weeks pregnant in places other than the airport right?"

Bubbie: "*TSK.* I'll get a wheelchair for everywhere we go. I'll buy one! What do I care?"

If I did agree to her outlandish wheelchair offer, she would have followed-through or at least died trying. If I requested a rickshaw, she would have bought a rickshaw, probably two. One to cart me around, and the other so I'd "have it for company." Because to Bubbie, excess is justified when disguised as preparation "for company."

Having raised her own 2 sons, I think she was silently pining for a girl. "Oygch!" (A modified use of "oy" counteractively used as an onomatopoeia for one's kvell), "Oygch! Can you imagine what I'd do with a girl?? Gawd. There's no END!" I was happy to learn the baby was a boy. Anxiously removing a Bubbie-purchased tracksuit with a sequined adjective printed on the rear would've been difficult to do politely. Nevertheless, baby's boyhood did not come without its own material challenges. Although buying new clothes for an unborn grandson is certainly not unusual, buying yellow duck footie pajamas with duck feet on the "footie" part is:

Sharon: "You know we're having a boy right?"

Bubbie: "What are you talking about?"

Sharon: "It's asexual yellow with ducks. You're secretly wishing for a girl."

Bubbie: "Oh stop it. Is that so wrong?"

What was next? A foppish Victorian boy suit with rounded collar and a powdered wig? Some rouge? Maybe she misheard, "It's a boy!" and thought she heard, "Pick a toy!" "What a joy!" or "No more soy." I'm not so sure but as always, she meant well.

Come Boy 1's 4-month birthday, we returned for yet another visit (with fight) to Bubbie and Zadie's house in Orlando. Husband and I were exhausted from the flight, its 2-hour delay and the arguments about who was going to hold the screaming baby. I had a headache behind one eye with such intense throbbing, I think it was visible to anyone looking at me. An inch of smut from multi-climatic airplane air was crusted on my face and all I wanted to do was scrape it off with a putty knife, pop some *Tylenol* and pass-out. As we walked into their dark living room, Bubbie flipped-on the lights to illuminate a huge, toy horse, the size of a Shetland pony. A relatively normal purchase compared to the battery-operated *Land Rover* given by yet another stranger cousin. When you pulled on its reins, a startling "NEEIIGGHHHHHWHHHIINNNEEEYYYYY" pierced through my forehead and could have easily evoked seizures in the neuro-sensitive; what it really needed was a warning label. My duct tape muffling method was rendered useless, because the speaker was so deeply located in its poly-filled torso. However, it was the pony's offshoot that bothered me the most: a button down western-style shirt, chap-esque jeans and a cowboy jacket with a giant lasso-spinning monkey appliquéd to the back. In fact, I think cowboy-monkeys were appliquéd onto each piece of clothing, but it was the huge one visible from Beirut that captured my attention the most. I'm sure a zillion-dollar, ten-gallon hat was also purchased but either forgotten or confiscated by the bank:

Bubbie: "Look at what I got for Tottie!"

Sharon: "What in God's name is that?"

Bubbie: "Isn't it cute? Son, I got it from that boutique that your cousin owns. You know, the woman? I had to buy something from her."

Sharon: "There's no way he's going to wear that."

Bubbie: "What are you talking about? Of course he is! My little Tottie monkey."

Sharon: "Nope, please take it back."

Bubbie: "I can't take it back!"

Sharon: "Your cousin won't take it back?"

Bubbie with sing-songy voice leans into the baby carrier: "No. It's absolutely adorable! My little Tottie-mutchkie-putchkie, we're going to wear it togeeeetheeer and we won't tell Mommmyyy..."

Sharon: "Oh, you have a monkey costume too?"

Bubbie, still leaning into the baby carrier: "The what? Theee what??
The whatthewhatthewhat?? Little Tottie. Oygh! I'm going to eat you! On rye bread! With some mustard! I just can't staaand it!!"

Sharon: "There's no way he is dressing up like Brokeback baby."

Bubbie: "Brokeback what?"

Husband: "Mom you're being ridiculous. Ok, let's go, I'm hungry."

Zadie: "I agree. What were you thinking? Well if you'll excuse me, *Publix* is selling coffee in dented cans for 25 cents each."

Of course there's an appropriate place for monkeys on infant boy clothing, but this disaster belonged in Dante's *Inferno*. I honestly don't remember what became of the circus monkey costume. Maybe it found its friend; the baby rainbow yamaka and they ran away to "I don't know what you're talking about land." I like to think that Bubbie showed it to a friend who validated my opinion. All I know and cared about is that I never saw it again.

---

* "Obvious Child" by Paul Simon, 1990

CHAPTER 4

*Spirits in the Material World

ometimes, I want to shake old hippies. There - I said it. Old hippies. People living according to the sensibilities and lifestyles of 1960s-1970's counterculture and failing to adjust to current day. Please understand that I am not referring to the grown-up hippies who still embrace the flower child dream. These people take the best of their past hippiness, blend it with a modern *Chico's* wardrobe and live as progressive contributors to society. They make great neighbors, social workers, professors and owners of marijuana dispensaries and spice houses. But I find myself concerned about the tiny segment of folks who missed the bus to evolvable social assimilation. You know, the people who look like they've been trapped in a time capsule for decades with opiates as their only source of nutrition or those comfortable leaving a gamey fog behind as an innocent bystander is about to eat an overpriced Caprese sandwich…. Sigh.

Do the ghosts of hippies past not realize that their musky selves at 20 are no longer charming at 65? Especially since they hardly were in 1969? Do they not know that ankle-length grey dreads on Grandma can trigger their grandchildren's nightmares? Sure, they're harmless people and in their time were the Vietnam era's human-rights activists and peace opportunists. But we've known that for many years and they've earned their peace medal. My old hippie friends, "the war" is over. Must we harp on it? Don't we have other politics to worry about? How about some vanity? I bet you clean-up well, don't you want to get invited to your granddaughter's bridal shower? "The Man" didn't go anywhere and has spawned even bigger corporate giants. This includes an enormous chain of organic food markets where, depending on the location, I've seen the spirits of Woodstock choose to hang their hats. I think they get free food but hey, we all have to sell-out sometimes. I do believe in "live and let live" and "do unto others" as decent philosophies toward dealing with people. But if I was walking around dressed in a pickle barrel, smelling like a farm and droning-on about Saigon, I sure as hell hope someone would smack some sense into me.

Think about the "flappers." Much like the hippies did to the 1960s, these women threw a cherry bomb into the Victorian era's social more mailbox and did not worry about getting caught. They challenged stodgy, old gender roles by personifying their "out with the old and in with the new" social movements through open expression of radical lifestyle choices. Granted the idea of "radical" in the 1920s meant: wearing drop waist dresses, makeup, dancing the "Bunny Hug," drinking, smoking, tanning and "necking." This may sound like your typical high school freshman formal, (substitute "my uncle's coke" for the "Bunny Hug"), but to the ancient people over 30, it was downright social treason. An entire era revolved around rebellious young women, even teenagers, who decided "to hell" with unwritten rules. They lived full lives on the edge and ran around like drunken sluts in the name of women's rights. Hell yes it caught on, the Victorians were outnumbered and the flappers made history.

My guess is once you flap, you never go back to the old way of thinking. So when The Great Depression hit, our flappers applied their newfound unconventionality and tenaciously did what was necessary to get by. You didn't see aging flappers running around the bread lines with fifths of whiskey tucked in their garter belts going on about "the cat's pajamas" and "petting parties." They didn't scavenge just enough money for rationed fabric to make ornate hats. These gals were too busy schlepping blocks of ice home for dinner and trying not to die. Once World War II broke out and the Depression waned, our flappers became poster girls for throwing themselves into the war effort and working even harder when they got there. Familiar with the iconic "We Can Do It!" poster? The one of a young woman flexing her bicep like a dude, with finger waves hidden under her bandana, glossed lips and perfectly arched eyebrows? She was the pop cultural image of the time and represented the evolution of the flapper into a more valuable and smarter version. Old hippies, why not follow suit? The times they are a changing right? I am not suggesting compromising your fundamental beliefs or becoming golf partners with "The Man" but appropriate mental aging would considerably increase your approachability factor, if you didn't smell like skid row.

Today we have baby hippies; the new generation of not-hippies because they were born in 1990. Do we call them: "pseudo-hippies?"

"hippies-redux or light?" "postmodern-Peter, Pauls and Pauls?" Consider a majority of the checkers at "The Man's" organic food markets I just mentioned. Not too long ago, I placed over a half-dozen items on the checkout belt at one of these stores:

Checker: "Hi how are you today?"

Sharon: "Fine thanks and you?"

Checker: "Oh I'm great! Are you having a good day? What do you have going on this afternoon?"

Questions like this are part of their job description and they really don't care how we are. Can we stop this madness?

Sharon: "Um, sure and not much, other than blocking-out the ocean of screams my house has become."

Checker: "Totally. Do you need a bag?"

Sharon: "What?"

Checker: "Do you need a bag or did you bring your own? We give you 10 cents off per bag saved from ending-up in a landfill."

Sharon: "Well, where would I put these things if not in a bag?"

Checker: "How about your pocketbook?"

My pocketbook? 10 cents per bag? Was this Colonial Pennsylvania? I looked into my "pocketbook" filled with a huge wallet, a pencil sharpener I accidentally stole, half a Nutella sandwich, a spilled bag of Fun Dip and yesterday's mail. My pocketbook. His Great-Grandma must have been a flapper.

Sharon: "Nope, no room in there. Yes, I'll take a bag."

Checker: "Ok then...is **one** bag ok?"

A tornado would be ok at this point.

Sharon: "Yes, that's fine."

The checker proceeded to take 2 glass jarred items, put each in its own oblong paper bag (the kind you never reuse), and then placed them into the main paper bag. This was a precautionary measure. Should my vitamins and wine have spontaneously combusted on the way to the car, they wouldn't have contaminated my 12 shrink-wrapped, non-GMO pretzel snack packs.

Sharon: "So, why the extra bags?"

Checker: "Oh we're supposed to do that...Would you like to round-up to the nearest dollar to feed a family of 20 in a remote corner of Tunisia that may be under water in six weeks?"

Sharon: "Sure. Gahaed."

Checker: "Would you like to save the 'conservation dependent' elephant shrew by pressing the red button to donate $5?"

Sharon: "No."

As lost-in-space as some old hippies can be, they at least have a solid source for their behavior. The neo/pseudo-hippies can't hold a one-hitter to the justification earned by the real McCoy. Sure there have been protest-worthy issues since 'Nam, but compared to the original hippies in their prime, have the neo-hippies broken any ground for social upheaval? Do they stand for causes the general public knows about or can remotely relate to? Not really. Maybe the checker should have asked:

"Would you like to donate $1 to feed our token homeless guy who hangs out in our parking lot? In one of Chicago's most affluent suburbs? Yep, Bruce, that's the guy."

or

"Would you like to round up your total to the nearest $1 to provide breast milk for local newborns with mothers too depressed, medicated or drunk to make their own?"

or

"Give a sum of your choice to support the 'Stop Talking So Damn Loudly On Your Phone - This Isn't Your Living Room Task Force?' People get burlap sacks thrown over their heeeaads.....huh? Come ooon."

Now those causes can change some lives. But there is hope for the neo-hippies in the world of retail do-gooding. Recently at the same store, a 6-foot, 105-pound lad with stinky, beige beehive-style hair and 2-inch diameter earlobe holes, was at my service:

Checker: "Would you like to buy a raffle ticket for an Italian vacation? All the money benefits the Quadriplegic Byzantine Parrot Fund of Eurasia." (Something like that.)

When did the continents get back together?

Sharon: "No thanks. I like my parrots immobile. Save the crackers."

Checker: "Are you sure? Because it looks like you could really use a vacation."

He gets me, the consumer.

Sharon: "Really? Okay fine. But If I don't win, I get my money back right?"

Pause

Sharon: "I'm kidding you know."

Checker: "Oh, okay. Do you need a bag?"

Ok, maybe he doesn't get me.

I wanted to tell him "no." "No" and that he should pack $75 worth of groceries in his nappy white-boy dreads, film-reel-sized earlobe holes and juggle the rest to my car. But I said no such thing. These kids are merely fetuses wearing grown-up rose-colored glasses, made of recycled material of course. They're not impacted the same way Aquarius's children were with draft-dodging and dead brothers fueling their arson attempts. Stupid questions like, "Would you like to buy a $20 basket made of petrified buffalo dung by a woman from a land with no name?" or "Heading to *Lollapalooza* tonight?" to a customer holding her screaming newborn, are certainly asked via managerial instruction. At least they are familiar with causes beyond the *Land Rover* they've always wanted. Here's to the neo-hippies: may they use their "Man"-taught altruism effectively, never wear a pickle barrel or ruin someone's overpriced sandwich.

You Can Do It!

---

* "Spirits in the Material World" by The Police, 1981

CHAPTER 5

*Black Dog

I got my first dog about five years ago. He was a little old man named Billy who stank to high Heaven from the moment we met. Sure bathing him tempered the stench for a day or two but when that warm refrigerator scent abruptly hit my nose, I'd find Billy just few feet away, shuffling off to a place he couldn't remember. Innocently he'd waft swirls of brown funk in his wake as if his body was asking for another bath unbeknownst to his brain. But I loved my stinky dog warts and all. No really, he had warts.

It was 1977. The death penalty was reintroduced, it snowed in Miami and my family got a cat. For many valid reasons, Mom was not big on animals in our house. Her only pet as a kid was a bird named "Bing," as in Crosby, the Christmas carol king. She attributes Bing's demise to a heart attack caused by one too many of her landlords' ear-splitting arguments. Was there an autopsy? How did they know what killed ol' Bing? Nevertheless, as far as "first pet" experiences go, Mom's was not optimal. It didn't help that a bloodthirsty hound chased her home from school on a daily basis. "That evil dog barked and chased me from 83rd and Damen to 80th and Wood *every day* after school," she told me. For all I know, she could have been chased by "Snuggle" the fabric softener bear, but that made little difference considering her small size. Back then, the Chicago Catholic schools' answer to overcrowded classrooms was to move the smarter kids to a room with extra seating and that was the extent of it. This left Mom practically a toddler in 3rd grade and "Snuggle" a monstrous, hungry threat waiting for her in the alley. You'd think riding the bus was as option, but understand the popular sport of the angry nun-teacher other than swatting students with a yard stick; any kid suspected of having bus fare rattling in her pocket could expect an upside-down shake from "Sister Lucy Fur" until she heard the satisfying *"ping"* of dimes hitting concrete. So the bus just wasn't happening for Mom. Did she prophetically see the dog chases of '48 as her own pet issues? Could she just not shake ol' Bing? Either way, the memories were enough for her to say, "hell no" to a dog.

A cat never attacked Mom, but Dad loved telling stories about his unapproachable, scratching and biting childhood pet "bobcat" Mickey. I believe "feral" was the accurate classification for Mickey, because I don't think there were too many bobcats trolling around Chicago's southeast side. Although "bobcat" *was* an effective clincher every time he had to repeat these stories to his stupid children. Years before I was born, he tossed Mom the idea to board a stray, grey tabby he inexplicably named, "Marina Cat of the Streets," but she tossed it right on back. Don't get me wrong, Mom loved cute, fuzzy things more than most. She just knew adopting Marina meant acquiring a chronically shedding, nonverbal dependent that could whine relentlessly, lick the salt of your pretzels and throw up every day before she'd have to leave for work. Given both their histories, we were lucky to ever get a pet; but after living five years with three badgering children well...Mom finally caved.

Riding in the backseat of my parents' car, Brother on one side, Sister on the other, we were heading to the local Humane Society to adopt our new pet. "Let's get a dog!" I said, but given my tender age of 4, my voice didn't travel too far. So I tried again. "Let's get a dog!" "NO!" they said in unison, "CAT!!" When we finally arrived, Dad showed me our new, tiny orange-furred tabby while he scratched her nose through the cage's slats. "Do you see how she's an orangish color? Like the color of cork right?" With a frozen smile I agreed, but knew nothing good was coming from *this* clue. "So we're naming her *Corky*." God I hated that name. *Corky*? *Corky* the cat. Well that just rolls off the tongue like a tack doesn't it? How anyone could associate this fuzzy kitten with something as practical and uncute as cork still eludes me. I probably would have named her *Mittens* or *Samantha,* Sister would have named her *Scarlett* as in *O'Hara* or *Nancy* as in *Drew* and Brother would've wanted *Klinger* as in *M.A.S.H* or *Countach* as in *Lamborghini.* But Dad seemed proud of the name, so *Corky* it was.

Soon after the cat's assimilation to life at our house, *Corky* became *Kitty* due to vested pride in *our* call to *her* wild. "Here Kitty Kitty Kitty!" We'd yell for her to crazily run for the huge amounts of food we shouldn't have been feeding her. Clearly so impressed by this trick, we apparently decided the cat really should have been named the slang version of her species: *Kitty.* She was unofficially Sister's pet and the very definition of "indoor cat." She was terrified of the outdoors, sat in armchairs like a human, spoken to, spoken for, spritzed with perfume, dressed in scarves during winter and a rainbowed "Hawaii" t-shirt in summer. Because when permanently covered in fur, wearing an additional layer during summer makes perfect sense for any mammal. Unauthorized use of my socks for cat toys was encouraged. Brother would rub his face on her furry belly despite anaphylaxis and Dad used her as the butt of an occasional practical joke:

"Gasp! Look what Kitty did!" Dad said convincingly enough because I never heard him say anything like that before. "Ew, she pooped!" he added. I feared Mom's impending discontent to yet another cat malfunction, and then noticed Dad's facial expression suggested the same. I did wonder why he didn't just discard the poop like any other parent would, but my thought was interrupted when with complete seriousness, he picked-up the small, brown, pinched log, looked straight at me and ate it. My reaction must have transcended horror based on his unabated laugh. This was a genuine, from the pit of your stomach, high school or Army prank laugh. The kind that fills your eyes with tears, clogs your nose and keeps you awake at night. The only other time I heard him laugh like that is when I made a quick turn to the bathroom and smacked against the closed door like the lost Stooge. I was quickly relieved to learn he actually ate a Tootsie Roll and not cat stool as it was a little disturbing. I highly recommend trying it with your own children.

Unfortunately, Brother, Sister and I continued to feed Kitty like she pooped diamonds: "Strawberry yogurt? Look! She likes it! Give her more. Milk too! Cats love milk on cartoons and some cheese balls. Cool she's eating it. She loves us!" After feasting, Kitty would then lovingly lick Sister's chin and due to good timing convince her that cat saliva cured zits. This remains her belief to this day. Around 12 years down the catwalk of her life, Kitty weighed somewhere around 18 pounds and needed an extra-large litter box requiring a twice daily cleaning to accommodate the results of her hearty appetite. Eventually, her Rubenesque physique caught up with her in the form of feline diabetes that required insulin injections to keep it under control. Unfortunately, its administration was not consistently communicated among family members:

Mom: "What's wrong with Kitty? She's listless, Kitty?... Kitty are you ok?"

Sister sits on edge of couch crying.

Mom to Sharon: "Did you give her insulin this morning?"

Sharon: "I gave it to her around 8."

Dad: "I gave it to her around 7."

Mom: "You can't DO that!! How many times have you done that?! You're lucky she isn't dead!!"

Sister sobs louder.

Sharon: "Well...she isn't right?"

Brother: "Didn't Sharon kill Auntie's dog a long time ago by feeding it too many marshmallows?"

Sharon: "No...*you* fed her marshmallows genius. I was busy watching Cousin cut a wart off his knuckle with a pocket knife."

Dad: "Oh sure, I remember that dog...well, I've got some soffits to replace."

Never wanting to "stir the pot" of a bad situation, Dad would escape to the garage, roof, crawl space; wherever he'd install soffits - or any hardware for that matter.

That day, Kitty's blood glucose eventually returned to its normal level. Not sure how Mom managed this, but I imagine the smell of a freshly opened can of tuna made Kitty alert enough to finish her *Lucky Charms*. Sadly, by her 18th birthday, she was a wasted, shriveled mess of a diabetic cat. I think Kitty knew if she floated toward the light by her own choosing, Sister would've melted and absorbed into the Earth. So she just carried on living: constantly shivering, unable to walk on her own, maybe she'd scoot across the floor a little, but that was about it. Mom spent a morning following her around the living room while she took pictures. I can still see her walking on her knees as she wept and snapped, wept and snapped. I asked her what the point was given the fact that we already had plenty of pictures of Kitty in the physical form we'd have rather remembered. I don't recall her response, as she was busy trying to not drown in her own tears. Although years later, my *own* dying cat lived in my closet and I also found myself taking pictures of her jaundiced, withered shell hunched behind a pile of untouched treats she'd usually take-out an Akita for. But there I was snapping away. Makes little sense but seemed necessary at the time.

When you've shared a small glass of water on your nightstand and spooned with your pet every night for years, it's hard to recognize their aging. But when house guests begin to complain and you know it is past time to let Fluffy go, it can be quite devastating. For Sister, devastation better describes butterflies pinned to Styrofoam on display at the library, than euthanizing a pet. There are no words. Luckily, I was away at school during Kitty's quietus, but the rest of my family braced themselves for Sister's reaction. Because her sensitivity level transcends the capabilities of 99.9% of Earthlings, it takes so little to make her cry. Give her *any* children's story, be it about a bullied cartoon cockroach or a vulture's lost dreams and expect a breakdown. But every emotional yin has its yang I suppose. (Meanwhile, my chiropractor shoved a probe into my armpit and said, "Most people are jumping-off the table at this point. You have a very high pain threshold.") Sister's tear inducers, at least the ones I can speak for, are as follows:

Song: "Puff the Magic Dragon" by Leonard Lipton and Peter Yarrow (emotions exasperated by book and cartoon adaptations): What's up with these trippy 70's children's stories that begin tragically? Little Jackie is mute from overwhelming self-doubt. Nice. Along comes a dragon from the confines of his psyche that transports the boy to dilapidated lands inhabited by personified playing cards, a giant pie-baking pirate and "living" sneezes. The boy can finally speak normally at the end, but Sister's inevitable tears are not out of happiness for the unmuted child, rather sadness about Puff and Jackie's separation. The creator denies drug references, but it's difficult to accept this plot as anything other than someone's acid-dropping flashbacks. Ok then, maybe this is what he saw while trapped in an isolation tank, but cry over this madness? Despite the child's regained ability to communicate, Sister still claims, "I'd rather be with the dragon."

Song: "Cat's in the Cradle" by Harry Chapin: About an absentee father and his "boy" who wants to be like him until he realizes Dad's a deadbeat. Adult boy deserts dad in a retirement community. He got what was coming to him in the end, so what's the problem? And where's Mom? With her "roommate" Pam again?

Movie and Song: "Through the Eyes of Love (Theme from Ice Castles)" by Melissa Manchester: About a figure skater who goes blind, slips on roses but finds love and fulfills her dreams. I cried right along with her, only because of the unconvincing plot.

(By the way, these songs do not have to be original arrangements. Porky Pig could sing them and still, instant waterworks.)

Movie: *Purple Rain:* Involves abusive parents, attempted suicide, dicey love interest and Prince's music, which is not particularly tear-jerking in the first place. The characters persevere in the end, the real-life Prince continued to be "Prince" and everybody made millions. (Wish I were a fly on the wall at *that* wrap party.) None of these facts made her feel better and to this day, Mom regrets allowing Sister (who was 18 at the time) to watch it.

Book: *Charlotte's Web* by E.B. White: Pig and spider friendship, bacon threat and spider death, wraps-up with baby spiders. No mention of babies' father. Tears understandable until age 10, but still going strongly at 50.

Book: *The Velveteen Rabbit* by Margery Williams: A boy loves a toy rabbit so much that he considers it to be "real." The rabbit is insecure because he has seams and knows that living and breathing rabbits do not. *(As a kid, this is when I'd stop reading.)* The boy contracts scarlet fever and in the name of disinfection, the toy rabbit is tossed into the garden to be burned. A flower fairy uses her tears and turns it into an actual seamless (*really* real) rabbit, to live in a *real* forest and there is no reunion with the boy at the end. Based on Sister's reaction to an estranged dragon, I accept her lifelong sadness but no one else's. It's a fairy tale, I'm sorry, get over it.

Book: *I Love You Forever* by Robert Munsch: According to her daughter, "It's the one with the kid near the toilet, on the cover," and one of many children's books Sister's 8 children do not "allow her to read." I actually found it in a bookstore's children's section and checked it out. Complete with illustrations, it begins with a mother telling her baby that she'll always love and hold him. Mom repeats this to her son throughout his entire life (like, all day and every day) as she becomes increasingly dowdy. First goes the makeup. Then she trades her contacts for tiny, *Miss Beetle* glasses. Her blonde, beachy waves are now a grey perma-bun and a *Little House on the Prairie* nightgown becomes her day clothes. Mom gave up years ago and must have guilted her son into dumping his "trashy" girlfriend to stay with her *and* in lieu of transferring to Singapore for that million-dollar promotion. She becomes elderly and the last page shows her grown son cradling his dying mother in his arms. Ugh. For some reason mom is wearing a hat, possibly to evoke thoughts of her chemotherapy? God almighty. What is this? I've never encountered a "children's" book so ridiculously morbid that it became funny. This book was sent home with Sister after the birth of her first child. Yep, Catholic hospital, "Our Lady of Perpetual Cutting." And they once banned *Huck Finn*.

Many moons post Kitty's death and well into my adulthood, I'd regularly visit a local animal shelter to see what pooches were available to fulfill my inner kindergartener's dream of dog ownership. There were about six cages where the smaller dogs were boarded and having no interest in a 110 pound Pit Bull rescued from an Alabama fight club, I rarely needed to look any further than those six cages. In the top cages were the token Chihuahua twins, bowel incontinent Yorkie mix and an angry Shih Tzu. On the bottom was a black, shaggy mess of matted fur with a protruding pink and black tongue. From what I could gather, the mess seemed happy enough so I asked to see him. "Billy" sat next to me on a bench and stared at me until he rolled over to show me his patchy belly for a rub I gladly provided. I'm not going to lie. Billy was old and so were his inborn accouterments. His "fur" was a conglomeration of nasty, nappy, mangy ropes that probably were home for a number of microorganisms unidentified by science. As he panted out of happiness, his halitosis was so paralyzing it could have taken down the Nazis. During his first dental cleaning, Billy's rotten teeth just slid out with barely any pressure and the slightest tug. I had vision for ol' Billy as the bathed, shorn, de-gunked and de-funked sweet dog o' mine. But not yet as the commitment was huge and I had other people to consider. I placed Billy back into his cage and shut the door only for him to immediately cry and attempt to grasp the slats with his stinky, crusty paws. Anyone leaving that dog might as well have hopped right into a hand basket with an express ticket to the underworld because the scene was just sad. "I'll take him!" I said.

As soon as Billy was introduced to his new house and angry cats, he comfortably hopped onto the couch like he came directly from another home rather than a shelter. It could have been Attila the Hun's home based on his condition, but nevertheless a home. "Time to take a walk and meet the neighbors Mr. Dog," I told him. "Oh," said one neighbor hesitantly, "wow.... what made you...do this? He's cu u-te." I know Billy wasn't exactly a prized Airedale terrier or insanely adorable Havanese, but he wasn't groomed yet and again, vision was a must. "That tail," said a particularly superficial onlooker, "that taaail." Sure, his tail looked like a dead shredded palm leaf. "He's a rescue. **A r e s c u e.** You don't pick-up shiny, golden, magnolia-scented puppies from the shelter. What's wrong with you people?" Susan, my friend and neighbor, came to take ol' Billy for a walk:

Susan: "I think you should name him *Luke*."

Sharon: "Eh, Husband's fourth cousin's name is *Luke*..."

Susan: "So?"

Sharon: "Well, we see him often. Oh hi *Luke*, this is *Luke* our destitute dog. He needs help just like you."

Susan: "What about *Jason*? *Jason* or *Jeffrey*?"

Sharon: "I don't like the name *Jason* for a dog. Besides, Rita across the street has a bicycle named *Jason*.... She so badly wanted to name something *Jason*."

Susan: "Well, what's her dog's name?"

Sharon: "*Charlie*. And *Jeffrey* should be a blonde boy, not a dog."

Susan: "What about *Billy*!"

Sharon: "Perfect!"

Susan: "Heeey *Bill…*"

Sharon: "*Billy.*"

Susan: "Heeey *Billy.*"

Billy was a little, feeble, wise old man of a dog. He had a hitch in his giddy up, cloudy eyes and the spirit of a wounded soldier. Senior citizens on the street would say to me, "It's so nice that you adopted a 9-year-old crippled dog. God has a place in Heaven for you." Although appreciative of the compliments, I honestly didn't see it that way. Of course I knew people weren't clamoring to get ahold of stinky Billy to surprise Junior for the holidays. His chance of surviving Christmas Eve in an air-holed container were dicey at best; he barely would've had the strength to drape over the edge of a gift box much less leap into Junior's arms without going into cardiac arrest. I figured Billy, at 9 years old, had at least 5 decent years of dogdom left and given his size, temperament and lack of shedding, why not bring him home? Unfortunately, he lasted 3. Billy spent his last year in a gradual yet arduous decline with no formal diagnosis to encompass his chronic incontinence, senility, shoulder pain, anxiety, depression, leg pain, overall malaise and blood in his urine. Living was painful for ol' diapered Billy and he was on every possible medication to treat symptom after symptom of a nameless syndrome specializing in his physical decline. His brain and body just had it. I'd hear stories of people passing out, running away and catatonic after having to send their dogs to bunk with the spirit in the sky, admittedly I thought they were a bit dramatic.

Well, I take that back and eat it for breakfast. From the moment we walked into the veterinarian's office until sometime in the future, I was beyond hysterical. I sobbed to a point where Husband's only choice was to stand there helpless and watch me like a train wreck from impact to unnerving, eerie aftermath. He stood on one side of the exam table, the veterinarian was on the other and I hovered facedown over a listless Billy teetering on the cusp between life as my dog and orientation with St. Pete. I knew I appeared traumatized as I tucked him in with his fuzzy, blue blanket and nestled his favorite squeaky bird toy under his paw. When my hysteria momentarily paused (due to my labored breathing), the veterinarian swiped the opportunity to say, "Are you ready?" I nodded "yes" but a couple seconds before the syringe pierced Billy's skin, I grabbed his wrist, looked up at him and said, "Wait! Are you... sure?" The vet closed his eyes and said, "Ye-e-sss." I think he was annoyed. Next thing I know, little Billy was gone and I was dog-less. I put my face next to his and cried like this was *Sophie's Choice*, scratched his stinky head and secretly wished for an impossible resurrection.

Yes, I cried all the way home and frightened my children by overtly exposing my emotional wounds. Have you ever witnessed someone express heightened emotion that made you completely uncomfortable? Not only because it was unexpected but because it was opposite of how you'd ever imagine or want to see that person? Like hearing a sweet, little old lady swear? Or watching your stoic gym teacher shed joyful tears while playing with a baby rabbit? At 11, I saw my Uncle cry at my Grandma's wake. He was a large, barrel-o-fun kind of guy, always boisterous and jovial, he'd throw Memorial Day parties involving an animal cooking on a spit and let me (at 10) drive around the neighborhood in a country club's permanently borrowed golf cart. That's how I knew him. But when I saw him bellow, honk into his hankie and drape his large upper body over his mother's tiny casket, the Earth seemed to turn the other way. I saw not my Uncle Jolly, but a vulnerable man in a state of raw grief. I was a bit uncomfortable, only because I felt like I was interfering in his private moment. Well, that's how I made everybody around me feel. "I've never seen you…like that," Husband said quietly before he ran away. He knew he'd have to pick-up my slack for little while, small folk would have to be extra good for Mommy and I knew I'd have to get over it fairly quickly to maintain order and serve as an example to my own people.

Those of you who have never owned a dog may not realize the impact of losing one, which is completely understandable. I live in my own personal frat house with 3 boys and Husband and have often considered building myself a secret home. Dogs don't say, "You're a little stupid when you drive at night," or bang on the table in the middle of *Denny's* over a delayed *Amazon* delivery. Dogs don't swear at televised football or play golf for days on end. They don't get disappointed when they learn you're a crappy cook or question whether you have the flu. They eat what you give them, tell no lies and a car ride makes for an exciting day. Dogs live for their owners and teach us selflessness. When they die, that effortless, unconditional mutual appreciation is gone. Bam!

I have since recovered and continue to browse the shelters. A year or so later, I adopted a 4 pound, black Yorkie mix with ears so endearingly enormous, "Yoda" or "Gizmo," were perfect names. However, I named her "Pixie" because she looked like a mythological creature from a historical sci-fi book. She was freakishly adorable and easily fit into a large purse. Unfortunately, she snapped at children who came within 3 feet of me and did not like the idea of making outside her toilette. I hired a trainer and gave Pixie time to learn, but given frat brother number 3's arrival was a few months away, Pixie had to find another home. Of course I cried when I returned her to the shelter with her pink blanket, tiny collar, heart-shaped tag and instructions from the million-dollar trainer. But my sorrow was quick lived. Not only was she immediately placed with an empty-nester librarian, her dogness was going to enlighten yet another soul in our human world.

---

* "Black Dog" by Led Zeppelin, 1971

CHAPTER 6

*Miss Me Blind

My siblings and I were not blessed in the vision department. Both our parents had adequate eyesight so I
don't understand what happened to us. Four decent
eyes from which to draw a genetic map and not one of us dodged
Blind Man's Canyon.

Sure, Dad wore glasses but without much apparent rhyme or
reason. He didn't talk about how "blind" he was or toss-out hy-
pothetical scenarios about misleading us to the attic during a fire.
Glasses-free, he'd safely use power tools, drive in a snowstorm and
caulk every gap in the house on Saturday, but then wear them with a
suit to a wedding on Sunday. He possibly was channeling a look, but
could not have desperately needed the specs. Mom too was lucky;
both her eyes, one nearsighted and the other farsighted, cooper-
ated seamlessly to provide her over 30 years of adequate vision. Yet,
down the road someone diagnosed them as inferior to bionic and
handed her a tiny puddle of a prescription: "Wear as needed." I have
no idea what that means. "Wear as needed?" I've always wondered
about the folks who, out of nowhere, "need" glasses at 24 years old.

I'm referring to those born after 1980 when people began to regularly check their vision from an early age without needing proof of a concussion. Past a time when an infant with glasses went from tragic to cute. What are they suddenly having trouble seeing today that they were perfectly content not seeing yesterday? If they "needed" glasses, they would have had them by now, so what made them think, "Ya' know, I'd like to see as many superfluous things with visual acuity as possible. Like air, Saturn's rings and the Prime Meridian."

"Oh gee Silas, dig the frames, why the change?"

"Well, my Dr. said it's a good idea to wear glasses while driving."

"Really Silas? That's funny, how did you manage to drive for the past 9 years? And graduate from Annapolis huh? Don't they reject anyone with less than a 95 percentile cranial circumference?"

No doubt, I envy people who don't require an electric fence should they wander outside *and* those who can safely drive a few miles before realizing they're not wearing glasses. It's just their occasional overreaction that gets me. Their barely-there designer specs are stored IN THEIR CAR like a hat or *Chap Stick,* but if misplaced, "Gasp!! Uh oh!! Where are my glasses!! I've had them for a whole week and now, I can't go without them!" Next is the mad search through the console, "Oh wait! Here they are! Hiding under the pilot license I earned a month ago. Woo! Thank God." Sporting them either with the urgency of a Stormtrooper or the delicacy of a debutante wearing Nana's tiara, they sigh in relief and drive off. The mere possibility of making it into a car much less drive without lenses affixed to my face, is inconceivable to me. But I'm no pessimist and make the best of my impairment. Sometimes while driving, I'll hold my specs above my eyes for a blurry second and ask myself, "Would I drive home without glasses for 1 million dollars? No." I've answered "No."

The second I remove my contacts, I "need" my glasses. If unable to locate them (or night guard, ear plugs, acupuncture tacks, breathing strips and bed remote), they must be found before time can continue. To the people who live with me: what if there was a fire? You want Helen Keller to be at your service? We say things like that. We have to. It doesn't matter if I'm 5 minutes from sleeping, I'll yank the comforter off the bed and swear until I find them, unless I fall asleep first. In which case, the youngest child usually locates them the next morning and even goes the extra mile to toss them on my chest to wake me. He knows if Mommy can't see, he may not be fed for a while. Really, it's a sweet bonding moment.

Let's review. If without corrected vision:

- You cannot determine the digital symbols on your speedometer as letters, numbers or pictures.

- Your eyes do not recognize the blurry figures darting through traffic as children.

- You're likely to miss that burning tire charging toward your windshield.

- You thought that leaping deer you hit was just smoke.

You "need" glasses to leave your house, to drive and you always have. Now that's a prescription.

For Sister, it took a couple broken fingers during her brief, yet steadfast figure skating career for my parents to realize not only was she a klutz, but one who couldn't see where walls stopped and doorways began. Mom loves telling the story of when Sister walked into the house wearing her first pair of glasses. Thrilled to discover our red shag carpet actually had texture and wasn't a huge piece of solid red foam, she leaped to the living room floor like a bored house cat to a fly. But like many 4-eyed kids, she refused to wear her glasses and soon crashed her green banana-seat bike, head on into a telephone pole. She was not hurt, I think because the wicker basket hanging off her handlebars served as a buffer. Who knew her obsession with *Dorothy* from The *Wizard of Oz* would have paid off like this? Dorothy wasn't myopic, she didn't wear glasses with inch-thick lenses. She was beautiful with perfect hair and awesome shoes. Am I saying that a girl wearing inch-thick lenses can't be beautiful? Yes I am, especially in Oz.

Up until age 20, Brother was a painfully thin kid who was always throwing up, allergic to everything outside and inside, along with most food staples and "anything with a fin." He required big, thick lenses that always reminded me of those dome-shaped map magnifiers you'd see in WWII films. The only frames sturdy enough were plastic tortoise shells that were about 4 inches wide as they were tall. I'll never forget one of his school pictures where his narrow, allergic head was weighed-down by these goggles, rendering him as a tiny mad scientist or even a small welder.

My introduction to glasses in kindergarten didn't stop me from recklessly propelling myself from the swings to intentionally land in dirt. When we returned to the classroom, our hot and dirty selves were instructed to form an even hotter and dirtier circle on a large carpet with the alphabet printed on it. I'm sure the smell was lovely and our little hands' nooks and crannies were flush with leaded soil, perfect for snacking on processed food to be washed-down with school-issued fatty milk product. We were supposed to sit on the first letter of our first names, but because another Sharon and I would always argue over the "S," we saved it for Sanjay, the ophthalmologist's kid. I settled in a corner near the bathroom and hypnotically watched the kids make their way in and out of the bathroom. "Can you see through those?" I heard. "What?" Although it may not have appeared like it, I did hear Miss Laura's question. I'm convinced we ask "what" to questions we've actually heard when we either don't feel like explaining our answers or hope for another question. "Your glasses, can you see out of them?" Apparently, at the time, I didn't wonder or care why Miss Laura, the teacher's helper, looked like a woolly bear caterpillar or remnant of a forest fire. According to my adaptable 4-year-old brain, navigating through the day by interpreting fuzzy shapes and decoding light fragments was good enough for me. What else did I need to see? "Give me those," Caterpillar said. Her attempt to scratch off the petrified sweat and dirt failed, so she resorted to washing them in the bathroom with soap and water. "There," she said, as she placed them back on my face. "Ooh, that's nice," I thought. "What were you doing out there during recess?" Miss Laura asked perplexed. "What?" I answered.

This was how it worked year after year. Mom brought me to the eye doctor, I'd botch the reading chart and attempt to pinch the

3D wings on a gigantic fly picture for him to confirm my eyesight was worsening by the day. Then his nurse would lead us to a stuffy, brown-carpeted room with about 4 racks of tragic kid frames to choose from. Tragic because back then, kids' glasses were ugly with no à la carte options such as frame color, thin lenses and overall proportion to your face. There wasn't a LensCrafters on every other street corner, and thus, so much like buying a sandwich from a vending machine, our choices were terribly limited. The frames were 90% functional (50% to see and 40% to hold the lens), and the remaining 10% allowed for gender specific colors and shapes: octagons for girls and huge squared-off ovals for boys. But glasses were crutches for the eyes. Needing them instantly tossed you under the "handicap" umbrella and it didn't help if your frames were brown or pink. They were often made of heavy plastic that slid off your nose and got in the way of important things like using a cup, crying and only occasionally served their intended purpose. For example, during my Confirmation, when the priest anointed me by drawing an oil-cross on my forehead with his thumb...my glasses were greasy and coated by the time I felt my way back to my pew. They were the size of dinner plates, where else was the oil going to go? I had never felt more pious, beautiful and slick.

Even adult, fashionable frames were horrible. Some had arms that didn't extend normally over your ear in a straight line, but dipped downward toward the cheek and then back up over the ear for an upside-down look. They were all huge with a light brown tortoise color or rimless with pinkish-brown gradient lenses. I remember seeing a picture of *Sophia Loren* wearing glasses, the upside-down-looking kind. To this day, when I see that picture I ask, "Why? Whyyy!" One of the most stunning women known to man and even her beauty couldn't shine through those things. It was like catching *Angelina Jolie* wearing her night guard. To me, she just looked like she had the flu or was going to sleep. When I finally took a stab at wearing hard contact lenses in middle school, the only time you'd see me intentionally wear glasses was when I had the flu or going to sleep. Otherwise, it was because a lens popped out of my eye and landed in some God forsaken place like the bathroom floor or on a cushion of dust underneath the bleachers. I wasn't one of those people who'd suck on this rigid piece of plastic, pop it back into my eye and be fine for 18 hours. Nope, I would've ended up with pink eye, so I wore my specs more often than I had liked.

Now, if an Italian starlet couldn't rock 80s glasses, where did that leave the rest of us? Not in Oz. So when I felt the need to look less dorky, I'd sacrifice clearer vision. A girl in my 8th grade class who didn't make the cheerleading team formed a "pom pon" squad; a place where cheerleading rejects, who either did not make the team or would never dare try, had a chance to obtain some blip of coolness on our middle school's social radar or at least be on the screen. Completely enthralled by this opportunity, my friend Jill and I didn't think twice about diving into the pom pon clinic and subsequent tryouts. Although the principal recruited the cheerleading "coach" (aka the Special Ed teacher) to front our gig, she had little to do with choreographing the tryout routine. My guess is that she was too busy grading papers and taking her 4 pm lunch break. It was the initial cheerleading reject, the spearhead of the pom pons herself, who created the dance that was going to catapult us into a whole new love for our gawky selves.

The routine was to the 1983 Billy Joel hit, "Uptown Girl." It was a squeaky-clean song with a 1950s feel that became a huge hit due to its association with the upcoming nuptials between *Billy Joel* and Supermodel *Christie Brinkley*. Perhaps it was thought that the whole "Uptown Girl" message would somehow transfer to how we presented ourselves or magically fool others, I'm not entirely sure. We practiced and practiced, sweat for the first time ever, knew the dance like it was etched into our brains and thought we were...awesome. When it was time to tryout in front of a panel consisting of: the slimy principal with a penchant for pre-teens who looked 25, the gym teacher with a heart of gold, and the overworked, under-paid and probably hungry Special Ed "coach," we lined up 4 at a time and performed for these people. Before it was my turn, I quickly took off my glasses and tossed them aside because pom pon girls didn't wear octagonal binoculars. The music started along with our bodies. Gazing toward the judges, all I could see were 3 human-like figures of various sizes and shades of beige. I knew who these people were, so I didn't think it was necessary for me to see them in detail. Eye contact? What's that? There was a part of the routine when we were to turn 360 degrees to the right then clap, and repeat on the left side. It was complicated, like walking. What I could see, were the people 6 inches next to me turning right when I was turning left and then turning left, when I was turning right. I was completely discombobulated by this discovery and therefore continued to botch the routine until the very end. Even though technically, one does not need to see clearly in order to tap-into a simple dance routine in her short-term memory, I'm apparently special and my lack of sight clouded that part of my brain. After tryouts were over, it took the panel about 2 minutes to decide that every person who tried-out made the squad. Probably because without every person, calling ourselves a "squad" was pushing it. I was very aware that my audition looked like something out of the Special Olympics and considering no one was cut, I knew we formed a pity squad. Was sacrificing a decent performance worth looking less dorky standing still? To end-up mourning the crumbling pieces of my delicate pride? For about 30 seconds, no it was not. But I quickly got over it.

Shocked given my mistakes, I asked Jill, "What were the judges doing while I was screwing up? Because I couldn't see their faces." "Nothing!" she responded. "The principal just sat there like this." She opened her mouth and slapped both of her palms on the sides of her face. We held hands, jumped up and down and screamed out of happiness. "Blaaaaahhhh!!!! Yyeeeahhhhh! We made it WEEE maDEE itttt!!!!" You may get a clearer picture of this staring-at-the-sun jubilee, knowing that Jill was at least a foot taller than I was. Should this spectacle have involved a hug, my face would have nestled in her bosom like a baby gorilla to her mother. Oh we didn't care that we wore old cheerleading skirts that someone dug-up from the bowels of the school. We paid no mind that their royal blue color was trimmed with white fabric oxidized to the color of dehydrated urine. We were downright psyched that the NEW part of our "uniform" consisted of a white t-shirt with the words, "Pom PONS," not the usual "Pom POMS," along with a generic all-red caricature of a toddler-esque cheerleader. While we knew either spelling was correct, why we chose the more awkward of the two, speaks volumes. We didn't care that half of us looked 8 and the other half looked like 16-year-old Mediterranean boys in need of their first shave or 8-year-old boys in need of their shave. And we certainly never picked-up on the fact that the principal practically had to threaten the Special Ed "coach" with eternal darkness in order to get her to manage (more like be present so nobody dies) the new force bound to rattle our school's social foundation to its core.

You see, we had pom pons, these glorious balls of shiny, red and blue streamers to shake around at will. The cheerleaders did not. All they had were the athleticism and agility to perform gymnastic-inspired routines that carried them to the State Championships, bodies that looked like they could breastfeed a third-world country, popularity, confidence and awareness of it all. What did we need that for? We had a love for Kenny Loggins's "Danger Zone" a la *Top Gun* and dumped our blood, sweat and tears into what we considered to be some stellar moves for the next home game. We were happy with that.

* "Miss Me Blind" by Culture Club, 1983

CHAPTER 7

*Smells Like Teen Spirit

Middle school is generally an uncomfortable time in one's life, given the fact that kids are wallowing in some variant of puberty, or in my case, waiting for it. As if it wasn't enough for unassuming young people to deal with ambushing hormones, the mid-80s was a particularly distressing time for any middle-schooler to have to appear in public. I think the generally unflattering clothing, hair, vision and orthodontic choices was karmic punishment. Payback to the parents who used hallucinogens, lit a pile of draft cards on fire or pillaged and looted during wartime. Our greater power was left unamused:

Dear Parents of 1,980-something A.D.,

"Ha! You think tipping-over squad cars and burning perfectly good bras was a way to 'give peace a chance?' All those drugs and freeee looove? Making your hard-working parents worry so much that they caught pneumonia and died? Huh??? Was the Great Depression not enough for them? What kind of stewards of my

mysteries do you call yourselves? This is shame. You shall pay. You shall pay when your already awkward, pubescent daughters irrationally cut their hair into the shape of squat, evergreen trees or whatever Dee Snider's hair shape is. Appearance will be the only thing that matters to your 13-year-old, so if she's built like a preschooler, her only choice in clothing will be the toddler department at JC Penny or the Cinderella Shop which fits up to a plus-size 8. Otherwise, they will have no choice but to dress like uni-browed traffic cones. By 18, they'll finally realize the lunacy behind all that neon and blame you for everything.

I'm sorry, but I've kibitzed with some of the Hindu gods and that whole Karma thing makes sense. For those of you who did not participate in any riot-like behavior, unfortunately your peers ruined it for you. I wish you much luck."

Love always,
God
P.S. Have a great day!"

I think middle school was when I made the friends with the longest shelf life. Everybody was so badly assembled in mind, body and spirit that our friendships bloomed from our worst selves. The "style" limited our look to either large toddler or brightly lit, preteen "ho" and made almost nobody look good. Really, the only controllable aesthetic competition at that time was who can wear more makeup and tease their bangs higher. Otherwise, most girls were playing on a fairly level field. No one waxed anything, forcing many a brunette to favor Bert, the angry pigeon-loving Muppet from the *Sesame Street* show. The *Clarisonic* was not invented, leaving our foreheads a rival to a major oceanic oil spill. Thank God we had Retin-A, which took care of the acne by chemically burning-off the top layer of our skin. Wanted highlights? You'd spritz your hair with *Sun In* (hydrogen peroxide) and learn to love that brassy, volcano-kissed look. Electrolysis treatments were only for wealthy people. If you did not want to look like a *Mario Brother* or a Persian cat, you'd use *Drano,* disguised as cream, to singe-off your facial hair (Retin-A only burned skin.) If left on 10 seconds too long, you went to school the next day looking like a spider monkey with a chemical burn. Now, please do not misconstrue. Of course personality is what ultimately draws people together. But humans are visually stimulated creatures who initially rely on appearance before diving into values, sensibilities and character. Unfortunately for your average middle-schooler, the buck stopped at, "Her boy-short, mom-given perm is about as mortifying as my mustache that I bleached to a patchy and rusty orange. I think I'll sit with her at lunch for the rest of my life. Wait, here comes the mullet with the headgear and insanely tight *Wrangler* jeans with the suffering zipper; another person with whom we can commiserate. We'll figure out if it's a boy or a girl later."

Pom pon Jill conveniently lived across the street with her mother and stepfather. Not only were we victims of history's ugliest and most unforgiving decade, she at 5'7," and I at 4'7," looked ridiculous together. One blustery Halloween, we decided to go trick-or-treating. Nothing odd about that except Jill was dressed as a giant clown and I as a giant baby complete with giant pacifier (see front cover). I should have dressed as a baby clown. At least then we would have made more visual sense. Back then, troubled kids attacked dorks with shaving cream strictly out of malice. This was neither planned, nor in a designated location with chaperones. Luckily neither of us was targeted as the attackers probably thought we rode the short bus and decided to leave us alone. We've been friends ever since.

In compliance with a relatively standard custody agreement, Jill's stepsister Linda would visit her father about every other weekend. She was our age, easy to get along with, her maturity motor was parked on our level and rounded-off our circus of the bizarre. We spent many Saturday nights using Dad's worn, black leather-encased "work tape recorder," to capture spoof interviews of: our 400-pound science teacher, Oprah, a known high school "drug lord" and anyone we considered fair game. Laughing ourselves to the failure of our faculties, we'd then unsuccessfully deny that we peed in our pants and this is how we regularly entertained ourselves. We'd recruit our parents to bear the fruits of our labor. I wonder if they found this activity pathetic enough to consider an intervention, but what were the alternatives? "Why don't you kids go loiter at the *White Hen* and steal some of those flying saucers for me? You know the ones that taste like Communion wafers? There must be some cheap beer waiting for you in the woods. Ya' know, the 'haunted' ones?" Or maybe, "Don't any of you have a 20-year-old boyfriend to meet in his van?" Our dorkdom must've helped them sleep better at night.

In a simpler time before cell phones, Facebook and a cyber-cloud forming its own dimension, people of "importance" used pagers to be contacted. We sophisticatedly referred to them as "beepers" and as long as it was turned-on and clipped to one's *Sansabelts*, it was a fairly simple system. You'd dial a series of numbers, then your callback number, the receiving pager "beeped" and either your obstetrician or drug dealer called you back. Doctors wore pagers for obvious reasons, but if a teenager was sporting one, his peers instantly assumed he was a drug dealer. The young suburban dealer could also be identified by wearing: MC Hammer inspired pants, a coiffed mullet, the scent of *Drakkar Noir*, driving his cousin's Mustang and about 17 years of life to speak of. Now this caliber of "dealer" did not have packs of destitute females muling balloons of heroin from Central America. He did not employ a thug named *Spear* to orchestrate enormous cocaine heists via blimp. They were kids who sold dime bags of oregano out of a pizza parlor or an under 21 dance club we always felt beyond fantastical frequenting. Their parents tended to be relatively well-heeled from owning a string of used car dealers with names like *BadCreditzCarSalez* or *EroLuxMotoShoppe*. Did Dad slip a beeper into Lil' King Pin's stocking last Christmas? Leave it on his pillow just to say, "I love you?" I'm not sure. Any beeper could have actually been a rectangle of licorice for all I knew, but in our minds, a pager equaled drug dealer period. It was more fun for us to see it that way and perfect fodder for our Saturday night circuses.

One of my favorite recordings from this time was our version of a heart-warming children's Christmas song about a lovable snowman that suddenly came to life in order to bring the Christmas spirit to a town of downtrodden citizens. We created this piece as a dedication to our local teenage drug dealer/future used car salesman:

Frosty the drug dealer was a high and burned-out soul,
with a big crack pipe and a runny nose
and two bloodshot eyes sealed closed,

Frosty the drug dealer was as high as he could be,

but the children say he could laugh and play
just the same as you and me.

There must've been some magic in that old white dust he found,
for when he placed it in his nose....

You get the rest, ok maybe not.

Thankfully, our dark humor has been preserved well into adulthood. Without it, inappropriate laughing during a job interview, baptism and dinner parties despite our spouses' embarrassment would be impossible. Here's to a long shelf life. Please store in a cool, dry place - out of direct sunlight.

---

* "Smells Like Teen Spirit" by Nirvana, 1991

CHAPTER 8

*Pour Some Sugar on Me

"You eat like a two year old," Sister said to me, "you need to be fed every couple hours." I suppose there's some truth to that. Since early adulthood, I've required frequent feedings relative to other people my age. It's actually not hunger that gets me as much as the plummeting blood sugar that can follow. In the early 90s, "low blood sugar" became the lay-person's self diagnosis du jour. It's benign enough to not cause panic, rarely warrants proof through blood work and gives us reason to snack. While in a hypoglycemic state, one may legitimately need to separate from a 3 hour Alcatraz tour to forge for food, like salt siphoned from the Pacific Ocean. One may also just need a break. "Catch up with you in a few!" and then nap on the beach.

Picture this scene, as I like to remember: It's 1980-something, my siblings and I are gathered by the fireplace. Grandmother settles in her rocker to crochet and tell stories about when she first came to Chicago and discovered her very manageable endocrine dysfunction:

Granny in her kerchief,
my sister with cat,
Brother wearing dickey and a porkpie hat.
I sat near Granny,
with barely a care,
that the fire department soon would be there.

"Good Lord!" cried G, "What's wrong with you!
Your Brother had never opened the flue!
Go to bed now, we're speaking of food.
And keep down the Zeppelin you'll wake the whole 'hood!
There there now, it's just us girls."

Sister was obsessed with *Barbie's* pin curls.

"It looks like you'd rather go hang with your friends,
even though they don't talk and have plastic legs."

Sister scurried off with barely a sound,
excited to eat the *M&Ms* she just found.
At last! I was alone with "G" for the night,
to learn from her wisdom and keen foresight.

"Listen to me, not to be mean,
but you've got to make sure to eat your protein.
It was 1932
when I finally got here,

I ate coffee and pie everyday for a year.
One day I saw spirals in front of my eyes,
and collapsed from what some,
thought was excess Scotch rye.
A doctor said, 'Stop! This women's not drunk! Her blood sugar's low you no
good runt!'
Get her some ribs! Beans and rice too!
She'll soon recover from eating good food."

Ah. Good Times.

Her tales certainly explained my toddler-like feeding intervals - good ol' DNA. I know people who wake up at 6am, work 8 hours in a cube and eat nothing until 4pm. They're ready to chew off their wallpaper but until then, they feel fine. However, much like an 18-month-old, I'd be hysterical and unable to leave my house if left unfed in the morning and unfortunately, I've been 18-months-old my whole life. Years ago, when I had plenty of energy to prepare for a day of work, a seminar or anything that was inevitably boring and required being trapped for hours, I'd prepare snacks to keep my chemistry balanced. But when I've ignored my inner Girl Scout, the effects weren't pretty:

I was about 25 years old, sitting at a table in the hallway of a community college where I was racking-up prerequisites for my second degree in the bustling field of dietetics. I might have been killing time in between classes but more likely was in the midst of a sugar plummet and couldn't stand up. I focused on a pretty cone of light pour through a window and splash on the drab, gray floor until an incoming breeze from an open door caught my attention. I turned my head and saw a silhouette walking toward me. When it lost its shadowed disguise, "Oh," I thought, "There's David Silver." For those of you who may not know, David Silver is the name of a character from a television show called *Beverly Hills 90201*. It was in its prime for about 10 years before my sighting. I wasn't even imaginarily star struck like, "OH MY GOD THERE'S THAT GUY WHO PLAYED DAVID SILVER!!" For a few seconds, I thought a real, make-believe person was tooling through the halls of my community college. Did I think I was in the show? A "reality" show? My reality or his? By the time he passed, I realized I pseudo-hallucinated, stood up, brushed off my brain and high-tailed it to the nearest eating establishment for fear of seeing Pocahontas sitting on the hood of my car.

About 7 years later, when Boy 1 was charging through his "terrible twos," Husband and I were left exhausted, apathetic and constantly annoyed each other. During difficult times such as this, his solution was (and still is) to go to the zoo. I don't ever need to visit the zoo, but since he's observed on-their-best-behavior, seemingly unaffected families at the zoo before, he thinks zebras are magic and make all the exhaustion, apathy and annoyance go away. You see, merciless fatigue and its physical-emotional effects are the small print of parenting. Common discomforts that bordered on intolerable before having children like: hunger, waiting in hours of traffic, being locked out of your house in the winter and colonoscopies are greatly blunted after having children. That "ocean of screams" I mentioned earlier to the checker at the store? For a female, living with more than one male equals mayhem and I live with 5 including my dog. There's a lot of screaming in my house, so at this point in my life, a colonoscopy is practically a spa day. In fact, I'm getting one next week and I can't wait. I'm often too drained to feel the low blood sugar in the first place, much less prepare low-glycemic snacks for myself. Plus, if my kids see me eat, suddenly *they're* hungry, but only after fighting, whining and crying about it first. Mom wants coffee and some samples from *Whole Foods* and suddenly everybody's starving for cake pops? No. I'd rather go without and see imaginary teen actors. Besides, in a pinch, I could nourish myself with my own tears. But back to the zoo.

Somewhere between the angry monkeys and the nonexistent lion came the headache, sweats and what felt like my eyes crossing. By George, I felt 25 again. I realized I couldn't rely on Boy 1's graham crackers to get me through however long Husband was pretending to want to be there. I thought this episode was going to be manageable, but I learned that one's endocrine poltergeists aren't easily ignored. Standing about 50 feet away, Husband yelled to me, "Let's go on the paddle boats!" "What paddle boats?" I answered knowing what he was talking about but hoping he'd suddenly lose interest. (It's a family tradition you know.) "The swan shaped ones!" he replied. I couldn't help but wonder why on Earth he would ask me this in front of a child obsessed with transportation. I tried to convince Husband that Boy 1 was probably too small for the boats. "Just checked, it's fine!" Of course the first time he bothers to look into what he'd usually consider to be insignificant details is when it's to his advantage. Typically, acknowledging policies like a kid's height requirement for the Midwest's highest roller coaster or the recommended age to feed a baby a whole, raw carrot without the risk of choking is not his bailiwick. "Da boat! Da boat!" squealed our child.

I dragged my ass to the swans, sat down and attempted to pedal around a murky pond about the size of a grade school multipurpose room. Of course I got the bird-boat with one bum pedal that would only turn in small circles. Being my passenger, Boy 1 was upset and released a whine-scream blend that entered my ears and pushed my headache from my forehead, straight down behind my eyes, one of which began to twitch. I'm not sure Husband was aware this was going on, I think he was pretending to be on a yacht. Meanwhile, I was pretending the swan was broiled.

By the time Husband got around to us, Boy 1 switched to his swan for another lap around the murk while I headed back to land to starve. Boy 1's snack stash was gone and the vendors were closed so I began to rummage through my purse for any form of glucose, like a dirty mint or errant Snow Cap. Thankfully, I did not begin to see the imaginary, but twenty more minutes and the *Care Bears* would have appeared. I pulled out some *Listerine* breath strips, ate two and had some minty fresh breath. What made me think ingesting stamp-sized sheets of dissolvable plastic was going to help? Maybe I was just on the border of delusion and while my eyes saw green aspartame, my brain registered Swedish meatballs. I don't know. Thankfully, Husband was off the bird boat, read my visceral hunger signals (my hands hitting him) and we left.

The next hypoglycemic episode I'd like to share occurred last week. Ten years older from the *Listerine* incident and still, I must eat like a puppy. My friend and neighbor Susan went with me to a local "bead and jewelry exhibit" which essentially showcased just how cheap jewelry can be if all parts are purchased in bulk. What? A bag of 50 leatherette bracelets for $10? Twenty crystal-like rock pendants for $15? Fantastic! It was nice to take a break from our mid-day suburban partying, last week's Unexotic Spice Show threw us just shy of rock bottom.

We were there for about an hour when my hunger kicked-in but I figured I'd get something after the show. While Susan was conversationally engrossed with a vendor about glass blowing techniques, I thought I'd run into the adjoining room and grab some crackers and cheese (carrots, cookies and coffee) from a banquet table I noticed earlier. As I walked in, I saw 2 large jewelry cases, each with one unoccupied silent salesperson behind it. I reached for a plate, some crackers and was going for a lovely baby Swiss when I heard, "Are you part of the Bead Show?" I turned around to find a middle age man with slicked-back salt and pepper hair, pleated beige trousers, and a nervousness commonly seen in narcotic abusing restaurant managers. "Of course!" I said as if cognizant of the notorious cheese looters from the 2014 Velcro Show. "Those aren't for you. It's for a private function," he added. I wanted to ask him if the spread was reserved for the janitorial staff, because all the functions were shutting-down in an hour and he had enough cheese to feed Chicago's entire public school district. But I didn't. "Oh. So, this is a private jewelry function with its doors wide open leading to the 'bead and jewelry function' in the next room?" I was confused. "Yes," he said. I looked up at the customer-free salespeople hoping for one to say, "Oh not a problem! Help yourself, we're leaving soon anyway..." No luck. "Ok then," I said as I turned around and dropped the cracker back onto the tray. I wish I had a cup of coffee, I'd have spit it back into the cup and handed it to the guy.

I found Susan in the same place I left her, only now they were talking about viruses, as in canker sores and not computers. She can become engrossed in conversations about both, so I interrupted them:

Sharon: "They said the food was for a different function. A function for ghosts."

Susan: "What?" They didn't feed you?"

Sharon: "No."

Susan: "Well that is just ridiculous. We'll go get something."

Sharon: "No, just finish what you're doing."

Susan: "Ok honey. I'll only be a minute."

For about 5 minutes that may as well have been underwater, I looked around at more stuff I didn't want to buy. "I'll go find a vending machine," I announced to the air. "There are no vending machines," a vendor responded. "Crap!!" The glucose plummet was upon me and Susan was still deciding which plastic necklaces she liked best.

Susan: "What do you think, this one or this one? This one has vintage beads."

Sharon fades: "do yoU thinK AnyONE WOuld NOTICE??!"

I was so ready to leave or lay down in the lobby, but didn't want to nudge Susan from choosing what she really wanted. I wasn't compelled to hit her like I did Husband at the zoo, his search for that magic zebra to make our parental tensions disappear was annoying. If peddling around a pond in a goose boat were on his bucket list, I would have lay down somewhere, waited for *Good Luck Bear* to appear and allowed my liver to eat itself. But Susan was actually having a pleasant time, so, I slowly shuffled toward the exit and looked at the displays along the way. I stumbled upon a small table-tent sign taped to the top of a register. The words were partially blocked by a pencil cup. **"We give d nts,"** it read. I thought it said, **"We give donuts."** My brain was so happy:

Sharon's brain: "Donuts! See? They're here to help us. The sign says 'we give donuts.' Where are they? I want one. Is it for a private function?....*Discounts...'We give discounts'.....Damn it!*"

Clearly, waiting was just not an option anymore.

Now, understand that Susan doesn't "do" cheap. This is a woman who had never been to a *Dollar Store* or colored her 4 grey hairs from a box before she met me. She wears her blue mink to the butcher shop and that's how she rolls. The Bead Show was my idea, but she was getting caught-up in the novelty and what was she going to do with them? Wear them? I reminded her that the "Susan" I know wouldn't be caught dead wearing cheap jewelry, so she dropped the beads and we bolted. After we left, I felt a wave of relief when we exited the seal-tight building and flowed into a freakishly pleasant 60 degree Chicago, December day. I even pretended to live somewhere else, somewhere people actually want to film movies. During our walk to find my food, I explained my phantasm donut moment:

Susan: "You had a mirage?"

Sharon: "I had a mirage."

Susan: "What the hell is wrong with that guy not noticing your illness?"

Sharon: "Well, I wouldn't call it an illness…"

Susan: "What an asshole! You need to wear an emergency bracelet. You never know what can happen, illnesses can change like that!" (Snap).

Mentally hyper-prepared for disaster, Susan thinks everybody should wear an emergency bracelet regardless of the disease: reflux, anxiety, mouth sores, drop foot, crossed eyes, which would be a waste of a bracelet considering all you'd have to do is look at the guy. But this is the ironic charm that is Susan; if someone with brittle bone disease fell down the stairs, she'd have the guy splinted, imaging ordered, the lawyer called, all while stably cradling him before an ambulance even left its port. Oh, and with a deli tray waiting. Her flight mode is outstanding, but take her to a new grocery store and she's overwhelmed. If my cat's hungry, she panics but if my cat blew up, she'd fix her.

We went into a juice bar and I ordered something green and obnoxiously healthy with a raw, vegan, not-granola bar from a person with a cigarette-shaped probe through the bridge of her nose. Knowing her reaction (to the food, not the probe), I offered Susan a taste of both.

Susan: "NO way. That is nasty."

Sharon: "Just try it. It's a perfectly simple detoxing combination of produce. Yesterday you ate green frosting."

Susan: "What's wrong with that?"

Sharon: "It's lard and neon gas."

Susan: "It's vanilla made green, I eat it all the time and it hasn't killed me yet."

Sharon: "You didn't notice the barista with a railroad tie through the bridge of her nose, but my organic drink is giving you PTSD?"

Susan: "Your drink looks infected and her nose doesn't."

Sharon: "???"

Susan: "So she looks like an ox. I have plenty of doctors on speed-dial if something happens to her while we're here. Ew. I smell parsley."

Despite its comparison to puss, the green drink helped normalize my blood sugar, but so would've tree bark by that time. What is the dysfunction in my brain that allows hunger to so easily toss me into a haze? The irritable fog I understand, but seeing imaginary teen stars and believing a bead vendor was giving away donuts? I've asked physicians about sleep disorders, diabetes and psychotic episode to no avail. I've accepted these bizarre experiences as pies in the face, reminding me that my Girl Scout hunger prevention tactics are still necessary. Amazing what it takes, I should have seen the red flag when I began to swear in traffic again.

---

* "Pour Some Sugar on Me" by Def Leppard, 1987

CHAPTER 9

*Listen, The Snow is Falling

*I*don't understand the resistance from people with mild, yet annoying hearing impairments, to wearing hearing aids. Some get caught-up in the "old person" stigma but nowadays, hearing aids are so tiny and transparent, they're practically invisible to anyone paying little attention to you. Gone are yesterday's chunky, buzzing ear-trumpets you'd need a switch board to operate. No longer are they exclusive to the helpless, elderly folk we picture as *Tweety Bird's* Granny. Yesterday's audio-crutch is today's streamlined accessory for the older-young adult set who desire efficient hearing. Let's make this happen people and spare your future children the frustration and eventually writing books about it.

If not born with poor hearing, many people over 35 have endured enough nerve damage from over-the-top-loud musical performances in enclosed spaces to warrant a hearing-aid prescription well before retirement. Remember that post-concert tinnitus that rendered you deaf (except to your own heartbeat) for 2 days? That muffled hearing you haven't experienced since age 10 when you were pushed off the high dive and certifiably drowned for 5 seconds? Before finally surfacing? All nerve damage. Hearing loss is not just for Granny anymore. Much like poor vision in mine, hearing loss certainly courses through the sap of Husband's family tree:

Bubbie: "You do mumble you know."

Sharon: "You, your brother and Husband are the only people on Earth who can't hear me. Until you, I was always told to shut up."

Bubbie: "It's very hard to hear you, you know."

Sharon: "No...no it's not. You're related to the other naysayers so, I see a trend here."

Bubbie: "The *Costco* woman said I have zero hearing loss and made me return the trial pair."

Sharon: "She lied."

Bubbie: "She did not lie."

Sharon: "What happened to, 'What a pleasure it is to hear the Mahjong ladies across the table! No more *yes* nods and asking WHAT? WHAT?'"

Bubbie: "Ok ok it's enough already Gottenyu. What are you? The German train?"

Bubbie may have poor hearing, but I also think her reception can be interrupted. This happens to me, but I can hear so the results aren't as apparent.

Sharon: "So you take a right on Main Street, go through two lights, turn right on Oak Street and the school is on the left. Do not be on your cell phone or you'll be arrested."

Bubbie: "…Did you ever get a hold of that woman?"

I've told her I thought she has Adult ADD and that life would be much easier if she treated it with medication. She didn't like that too much.

Bubbie: "Are you crazy? I'm not jumping out of my chair all over the room like my children did at 6 years old!"

Sharon: "It's different in adults."

Bubbie: "What? Get out of here."

Sharon: "You lose your keys more than you find them. That's like… hallmark adult ADD."

Bubbie: "That is so rude!"

Sharon: "Zero intentions to be rude. You should read this book. It'll help you. I'm almost finished with it then it's all yours."

Bubbie: "Did you ever get a hold of that woman?"

Sharon: "See?"

Bubbie: "Ok fine I'll read it...."

Bubbie under breath: "ADD."

Bubbie forgot her keys, left with my book and I never saw it again.

On another branch of Husband's family tree is Bubbie's brother, aka "Unkie." He's a free spirit extraordinaire with hearing loss in one ear, a missing foot from a hunting accident and selective deafness. Anytime you tell him something he doesn't want to hear, he'll ask you to repeat yourself as if he either couldn't make heads or tails of your diction or you tapped Morse code on the mouthpiece. Buried within his curveball, is hope that repeating yourself will cause you to slap your forehead as you come to your senses and change your mind in his favor.

Unkie: "Hi Tot, (Tottie) I'm calling because I'd love it for you and the kids and Sharon if she wants, to join me on a canoe trip through the wilderness."

Husband: "Since when do you have a canoe?"

Unkie: "I found this great canoe I picked-up from a friend's house. You should see it. It's great and it's NEVER BEEN USED."

Husband: "Which friend? Did you just meet him and happen to stumble upon his yard sale?"

Unkie: "He's uh...an old friend from Wisconsin *(cough)* knew him from camp as a kid. Anyway, I discovered this fantastic lake about 30 minutes north behind that water purification facility."

Husband: "You mean behind the sewage plant? Isn't that where someone got water into a paper cut and eventually needed her finger amputated?"

Unkie: "Wait, hold on *(candy wrapper crackle guised as interference)* I'm having a hard time hearing and this phone is old *(tap, tap cough)*. Sorry, I was up all night. Counseling misplaced war veterans. What did you say?"

Husband: "Maybe try putting the phone on your good ear. Can't go canoeing."

Unkie: "What? Yes the leaves are beautiful this time of year."

Husband: "Still can't."

Unkie: "Oh... ok, well, how about we break bread later with a few buddies from my *Zen after 60* men's group? Great guys. Remember Marceau with the glass eye? And Louis? The guy with hair on only the left side of his head? Oy. He just got a free liver transplant. Can you imagine?"

Unkie holds his throat and makes loud, animated, choking sounds to express his relief from not having the same disease as if an emotional vaccine for his fear of chronic illness.

Zadie on the other hand, climbed right on the bandwagon trailblazing to the land of listen and finally surrendered to wearing hearing aids. "I know I have a very difficult time hearing high-pitched female voices, particularly in a crowd. This hearing aid is really an impressive product." Zadie loves the word "product." He could be talking about baking soda or a Ferrari, but if he has a positive commentary, its generic label of quality is "product." "I found this condensed balsamic glaze while in Galena with your mother; really a wonderful product." He'd never say, "Your mother seems to believe her new, pool-inspired inflatable buffet is a crappy product." Even as I write this, it feels wrong.

Regardless of compliance, he occasionally has difficulty hearing others who also can't hear, do not wear hearing aids *and* already speak loudly because of it. For example, if Bubbie or Unkie yell a question toward a hearing aid-wearing Zadie, he'll yell "WHAT?!" back at them. I don't know why, he should hear them. I'm not sure he's aware of this phenomenon; as Papa bear of the pack, maybe his inner caveman is attempting to shepherd family members occupied by their dwindling senses. This would be audibly more conducive for the average-hearing stock to listen for impending plate shifts or signs of the Apocalypse. Or maybe he just doesn't want to deal with what they're saying. Just a thought.

Bubbie: "DO YOU HAVE THE KIDS IN THE CAR?"

Zadie: "WHAT?!"

Bubbie: "DO YOU *HAVE* THE *KIDS* IN THE CAR?"

Zadie: "OF COURSE I HAVE THE KEYS TO THE CAR!"

Bubbie: "WHAT?"

…pause…

Zadie: "WHAT?"

That was it. I witnessed this exchange moments before they put my children in their car and drove away. There was no verbal resolution of missing or found keys, cars or kids or clarity established about what they were initially trying to tell each other. Maybe they figured it wasn't worth the bother. If it was that important, they would have yelled something else for the other not to hear.

Through family lines and over property lines, Susan's husband (Mr. Susan), 15 years her elder husband, should hitch a ride with Zadie on that same wagon. His situation isn't a matter of losing focus or social motives suddenly worsening his deafness. When he tells you he "can't hear you," he *really* can't hear you. "YOU NEED TO SPEAK LOUDER!!" He'll say as if angry but not. Sure, his volume can be unsettling for some listeners and if *your* volume doesn't match his, the conversation may abruptly end. You don't have to be a block away either, I've experienced this across 5 feet of kitchen table. As an equal opportunity loud-through-necessity responder, Mr. Susan doesn't discriminate. Whether you're Bambi or General Patton, his loud reprimand is one-size-fits-all and appropriate in any situation:

One

On Halloween during his younger deaf days, Mr. Susan would put on a ski mask, wait at the bus stop for the neighborhood kids and "trick" them with his verbal chainsaw imitation. Obviously, real chainsaws are louder but his version was terrifying enough. Imagine how loud a deaf chainsaw would be:

Susan: "WHY ARE YOU SO STUPID??!!"

Mr. Susan: "HOW WAS I SUPPOSED TO KNOW THEY WERE SCREAMING?"

95

Susan: "THE KIDS MOUTHS WERE OPEN AND THEY WERE RUNNING AWAY FROM YOU. WHAT DID YOU THINK THEY WERE DOING? YAWNING? WHAT'S WRONG WITH YOU!!?"

Mr. Susan: "I THOUGHT IT WOULD HAVE BEEN FUN FOR THE KIDS!!"

Two

Picture a summer day. Mr. Susan is standing on his front porch and I on mine.

Mr. Susan: "HELLO MRS. MEITIN WAS MACHST DU?"

Sharon: "Fine thanks, how are you?"

Mr. Susan: "I CAN'T HEAR YOU!!"

Sharon: "HOW ARE Y…"

Boy 2 runs toward a strange dog in the street, I run after him to avoid tragedy and yet Mr. Susan is still chipping-away at this conversation.

Mr. Susan interrupts: "LOUDER! YOU HAVE TO SPEAK LOUDER!"

I capture Boy 2 just before he attempts to pet Princess the Pit Bull.

Sharon: "I'M FINE!!"

Mr. Susan: "DID YOU ASK HOW I AM?"

Sharon out of breath: "YES!!!!"

Boy 2 and I make our way back up the driveway and to our front porch.

Mr. Susan in normal tone: "I'm well thank you for asking. MRS. MEITIN?" (Loudly again).

Sharon: "YES!!?"

Mr. Susan: "YOU REALLY NEED TO KEEP THOSE KIDS FROM RUNNING IN THE STREET!"

Expect to give about 5 minutes of your time to complete your exchange.

Three

Well into his 70s, he has no problem walking shirtless down the block to a neighbor's house and sitting alone on their front lawn swing, with maybe a martini in hand or maybe not. Eventually, someone would sit beside him for conversation, but it's not always entertaining for both parties. He once very loudly asked a neighbor currently on a teachers' strike, "SO MRS. GOLDSCHLAGER. EXPLAIN TO ME WHY YOU THINK YOU SHOULD BE PAYED MORE MONEY!" Intimidated by both his loudness and inappropriate questioning, a wide-eyed Mrs. Goldschlager could only muster a few, squeaky utterances in response. But to Mr. Susan, this was only a friendly test of wit that she failed, so it only made sense for him to try again. "YOU MUST SPEAK UP! NOW I'LL ASK THE QUESTION AGAIN!" Goldschlager panicked and ran home.

Susan: "I don't know why he feels the need to do that to people, I think he has antisocial personality disorder. In fact, I told him that."

Sharon: "Oh please. It's not like she doesn't know what he's like... she took-off like he flashed her in the supermarket. So what did you tell him?"

Susan: "I told him, *I think you have antisocial personality disorder.*"

Sharon: "What'd he say?"

Susan: "He said I hurt his feelings. Was he at least dressed when he pissed-off our neighbors?"

Sharon: "From the waist down, yes."

Susan: "Oh for God's SAKE! He's had every hair lasered off his body including his head. Look at him. He looks like a worm. An antisocial worm."

I've asked Susan why he doesn't use hearing aids, but the only answer she's ever given me is, "Because he's mental." They have a very special flavor of love. I can't speak for his mental status but I can for his eccentricity, which may have more to do with his disinterest in hearing aids than any insecurity about age:

One
He regularly scampers outside to retrieve the morning paper wearing literally nothing but his wife's unbuttoned, full-length blue mink coat, a pink, knit or baseball hat and depending on the weather and a pair of *Crocs*.

That's a lot of work to grab the paper, but I've seen him sport the coat in the summer, so there's evidently a look he goes for and not just a last minute need for warmth.

Two
The first time I met him, he said, "Hello, congratulations for paying entirely too much for your house." That's when I knew I liked him.

Three
Should he be alone during a power outage, he calls his wife and panics:

Susan: "Who does he think I am Zeus? I don't control the electricity. What is he worried about? The air conditioning? It's 75 and 10 am for God's sake."

Sharon: "Is Zeus the god of electricity?"

Susan: "Isn't he the one with the lightning bolt on the Peter Pan hat?"

Sharon: "I think you're thinking of the *FTD* florist guy."

Susan: "The what?"

I've since learned that FTD guy is the god Hermes, known for quickly and safely delivering messages between other gods. Apparently he's a cheetah at delivering flowers and his Peter Pan hat is adorned with wings, not lightning bolts. In case you were wondering.

What does a mind full of quirks have to do with poor hearing? Usually nothing, but in this case, the eccentric soul with the worst hearing acknowledges it the least and those with better yet still poor hearing highlight it through denial and selective deafness. I think Mr. Susan sees his hearing situation (if at all) as another tile added to his current mosaicked self. Mr. Susan with sharp hearing would be like a skinny Santa or a fat Gandhi, and that just doesn't work when seeing your missing pieces as parts of a whole.

* "Listen, the Snow is Falling" by John Lennon and Yoko Ono, 1969

CHAPTER 10

*The Ghost in You

Many moons ago, I was prescribed a medication to help me fall asleep and keep me there for a normal amount of time. Night one of my "treatment," I popped the pill, waited for the sandman and was zonked fairly quickly. That is, until about 3 hours later, when I found my eyes open, brain spinning and exhausted body unwilling to work together and deliver some quality REM.

Trying to fall back asleep makes insomnia all the worse so I thought I'd do something equally useless and fetch myself some water. I made my way toward the edge of the bed and froze when in front of my eyes were hundreds of *Froot Loops* staring at me. Phantoms they were, perfectly overlapped on my pillow like shingles. The vision jarred distant memories of the iconic *Candy Land* game board, which was weird because I never owned the game as kid and only occasionally played it at other people's houses. Averting my gaze upward from the *Froot Loops,* I saw a multicolored circus train - chugging away in the air above the foot of my bed.

Sharon: "Look!!"

Husband groggily: "Wha?"

Sharon: "Look at my pillow. *Froot Loops.*"

Husband: "What?"

Sharon: "You don't see *Froot Loops* on my pillow?"

Husband: "No."

Sharon: "Do you see the circus train in the air?"

Husband: "The what?"

Sharon: "Floating above the bed? I see yellow, red and pink box-cars...there's a giraffe, a lion and an elephant is pulling the whole thing. Right there. Don't you see that?"

As I continued to describe this, Husband made his, "Something unsavory is happening but I can't look away" face; he tightens the muscles behind his eyes as if squinting, while trying to keep his eye-lids wide open. The last time I saw this was when I was sick, as in, I-drank-the-Ganges-River-sick. Bent over the toilet wearing ancient, brief-style underwear, wool knee socks with "Iceland" print-ed around the top and a shirt drenched from marbles of the toxic sweat popping out from my pores, I was a vision. A puking vision.

What I technically had were "pseudo-hallucinations." In other words, I vividly saw the *Froot Loops* but at the same time knew they weren't really there, so I wasn't completely down the rabbit hole. Admittedly I was a little disappointed, if thrown delusions as a pharmaceutical side effect, it should at least feel like the trip of a lifetime well worth my exhaustion the next day. Otherwise, it's just a nuisance, *not* worth my exhaustion the next day. "Call your doctor tomorrow," Husband said before he turned over and fell back to sleep. When I looked down, the *Froot Loops* were fading away and when I looked in front of me, all I saw was the top of my armoire.

Recently I told this story to Susan. Naturally she was alarmed, but I was pleasantly surprised she did not suggest I wear an emergency bracelet. She proceeded to tell me about Mr. Susan's macular degeneration causing *him* to hallucinate only a few months ago, but instead of cereal and circuses, he saw "little people."

Susan: "I was downstairs when I heard him yell from the bedroom, 'YOU HAVE TO MOVE OUT OF MY WAY! I DON'T WANT TO STEP ON YOU!' "

Sharon: "Ok... then...?"

Susan: "Then what? I ignored him. He's always yelling about something for me to ignore, why should this be any different? He just kept screaming, 'MOVE OUT OF THE WAY LITTLE PEOPLE! I DON'T WANT TO STEP ON YOU!!' Then I heard this stomping. Shuffle, stomp, shuffle, shuffle stomp. God almighty, I thought the ceiling was going to cave in on me."

Sharon: "Stomping?"

Susan: "Stomping. Like he was either *trying* to step on the little people or avoid it. Who knows. I think he was making his way from the bed to the door, but couldn't find a place to put his huge feet because the imaginary people were in the way (eye roll). God forbid he gets out on the other side of the bed."

Sharon: "Maybe they were surrounding the bed and tying him down like the Lilliputians did to Gulliver."

Susan: "Well they can have him. *Then*, I think he tried to leap over them, because I heard something crash. Not him, maybe a lamp. Who does he think he is? Peter Pan? The world's oldest Peter Pan? Have you seen his feet? 'THE LITTLE PEOPLE WON'T GET OUT OF THE WAY! THEY WON'T LISTEN TO ME!' Ugh. Only *this* should happen to me."

Sharon: "Ok....??!!"

Susan: "Ok what? I'm going to check myself into a loony bin and swallow the key. That's what."

Later that day, Mr. Susan asked his wife if she saw any little people running around the house. She asked what they looked like but the only description he could give was again "really little people wearing casual, old-fashioned clothes." They weren't elves or evil sprites, just mini Victorians, trying to mind their own business.

Susan: "I actually felt sorry for him, so I told him Bea and Crayola were visiting him."

Sharon: "Who in God's name are Bea and Crayola?"

Susan: "My two best imaginary friends as a kid."

Sharon: "Like a B-e-e and a crayon?"

Susan: "No, like *Aunt Bea* and a crayon. They were always there for me Bea and Crayola…"

Again. They have a very special flavor of love.

Susan has yet to force either of us to wear an emergency ID bracelet engraved with something like, "Hallucinatory Disorder Not Otherwise Specified." However, if the *Eggman* spontaneously appears to either of us again, say, while driving on the tollway or lifeguarding a kiddie pool, she'll definitely have us shackled at the hospital. Thankfully, I haven't had another episode or taken prescription sleeping pills since my first and hopefully last experience. As for Mr. Susan, the tiny Victorians visit occasionally and prefer to run around his room in packs, but he appreciates that they're at least quiet about it. I suppose he's lucky to see only the little people, I read an article about a woman who thought her walls were covered in white fur. She tried to scratch it off and gave herself a nervous breakdown in the process. Another victim saw a *Barney the Dinosaur*-sized baby standing on his couch, something I have no doubt would give *me* a nervous breakdown. I can handle seeing tiny versions of typically larger things, but enormous versions of typically smaller things give me the willies. Ever stumble upon footie pajamas big enough to fit a large adult? Is this supposed to be cute? I've literally been unable to find footie pajamas for an 18-month-old but hey, my 6' 4", 300-pound mechanic is all set. I want to light these pajamas on fire because they are just so wrong. That being said, unless it can take stellar care of me, please God, no giant babies. The regular-sized ones are difficult enough.

---

* "The Ghost in You" by The Psychedelic Furs, 1984

CHAPTER 11

*Send in the Clowns

One of the few beauties of being 13 (and "a few" is pushing it) is the "live for the moment" attitude toward self-realization. Of course this is a beauty realized in retrospect; without years of experiences to draw from, you have no choice but to live for the moment. The average 13-year-old may not think to discontinue a conversation with an obscene phone caller from the county jail or be vain enough to forgo hammering half-dozen sliders before dinner and a nap. But as we mature, we sew our experiences together to eventually create the tapestries of our lives. Now, some tapestries may be strong, some beautiful, they can be ugly, disintegrate or even go up in flames, but regardless, it's interesting to reflect on some of those initial stitches.

"Look at all those kids singing," Mom said while watching some *PBS* Christmas special. "They're about your age, you should do that," she added hoping I'd say, "Oh yes! Let's find an agent pronto! Wait! Let me change my entire personality first." Instead she got, "Uh huh," or "Ok?" Once she informed me of a casting call for *Annie* and suggested I audition despite my lack of any dance, vocal or acting training. I had no desire to be a show kid. I could easily imitate one, but to actually "be" one required a certain persona and persistence that neither of us had for musical theatre. Mom would mention an opportunity she read about in the paper, I'd say "no" and for the most part, that was the extent of our climb up Broadway Mountain. So while other kids were attending academies for the arts and honing their crafts during every waking moment, Mom and I were drinking complimentary coffee in the mountain's lodge. I don't know why she thought I had a shot to be cast in a musical and as much as I appreciated her seeing any potential, it gave me the diluted idea that landing a part was remotely possible.

Every year, Chicago's Goodman Theatre presents the timeless classic by Charles Dickens, *A Christmas Carol*. A huge production with a significantly sized cast and ample chorus, it relied on Chicagoland's best to pull it off. It was the spring of 1987 and Mom saw yet another newspaper ad calling for kids of various ages to audition, which required nothing more than showing up on time and singing one Christmas carol of our choice. Considering *Bloomingdale's* grand opening was on the same day, I figured why not? It was a win-win. I'd go belt out some "Suzy Snowflake" for experience sake and hightail it to *Bloomie's* to revel in 1980s glut that we all so fondly remember. Of course, Jill and Linda were all over this opportunity, God forbid I do anything without my circus friends to make an ass out of myself right alongside of me. I don't think any of us realized just how legitimate this audition was, but it was a day downtown so nobody really cared.

The three of us perused an old book of Christmas piano music to choose our songs. For me, "God Rest Ye Merry Gentlemen" was a wise choice simply because I knew the words and I really wanted to drive it home with the "Criiiiiiist, the Looord" part at the end. Jill chose "Silent Night" also because she knew the words. An all around quiet song, since the desert, manger and Mary are arguably quiet things, its conservative pitch made it easier for Jill to use her small singing voice that had about as much variation as humming. Let's just say the crescendo and decrescendo were not her jam during that time in her life. "Jingle Bells" worked for Linda, because there weren't many Christmas carols about candy that didn't involve a complicated arrangement accomplishable by only Andy Williams. Great! We had our songs, so all we had to do is practice. Having taken piano lessons for years, we thought it was a good idea that I played while they sang. It would have been an even better idea if I had any clue as to how to be an accompanying pianist, or even a ka-zooist for that matter. As I attempted to tickle "Silent Night" on the plastics, Jill began to sing from what sounded like Canada.

Jill: "Siii lent Niiiight, Hoo…"

clink clink clink clink clink cl…

Sharon: "Wait, let me start again."

clink clink clink cl…

Jill: "Siii len---t --n iii…iight….aaall is caa…

clink clink clinkclink

….aalm, alll is

clin... Ok stop. This is ridiculous."

Sharon: "Why?"

Jill: "Because you're playing is so choppy I have to sing like, 'S -i - i - i ...le - nt N-i- -i--gh - t, -- Ho --- o - - - - oly Ni-ni-iigh-----t... ......
.... I'm done anyway. Do you have any *Suzie Qs?*"

She had a point. I don't remember hearing Linda's rendition of "Jingle Bells," but considering her singing and speaking were practically indiscernible, it's possible she practiced in my presence and I just wasn't aware of it. With the same recorder on which we brought our *Less Than Zero*-inspired "Frosty" to life, I practiced my carol alone in my room a couple times. When I played it back to myself, my ears registered that it was "loud enough," proceeded to tell my brain it was "good enough" and that was the extent of my practice. A few months earlier, we overpaid someone to record in a booth, our Karaoke to Madonna's "Dress you Up." The song begins with Jill and Linda's quiet meek tone with just a hint of scratchiness, "You've got style that's what all the giiiirlls sayyyyy...." beaten over the head with **"ALL OVER YOUR BOOODY ALL OVER YOUR BOOODY!!"** flying out of my mouth like a cannonball in a tennis court. I thought that was pretty awesome so, apparently I was ready for the Goodman.

It was audition day and I put on *Benetton's* best, green and purple plaid skirt with green cardigan. That's right friends, green and purple. Mom dropped us off at the theatre where we each received a number and waited in the lobby to be called. As I looked around the room, I saw our competition practicing scales, warming-up their pipes and rehearsing unnecessary monologues like show kid orphans hoping to be noticed by a director. I didn't find myself intimidated by the scene, this land was foreign for which I had no passport and little desire to learn the language. Jill and Linda went through their auditions quickly and I was up. Just like in the movies, there was a blinding light illuminating the stage, in front of which sat a panel of judges. They asked me the standard, demographic related questions along with a couple personal ones like, "What do you like to do on your spare time?" I could have impressed them with my ignorance of the trivial and said, "Oh... well I enjoy playing my great, great-grandmother's zither for the Alzheimer's patients at our state-funded old folks home." But honesty is the best policy.

Sharon: "Um well...I like to watch *All My Children* and eat White Castles."

Judges: "Ok greeeat. So what will you be singing for us today?"

Sharon: "God Rest Ye Merry Gentleman."

Judges: "Greeeat. You can start when you're ready."

"God Rest Ye...
....
....
....
............................."CHRIIIIIIST THE LOOOOOOORD!"

Judges: "Thank you Sharon, we'll give you a call if we're interested."

We hopped in a cab and headed to *Bloomingdale's*. Working our strategically mismatched threads and high, crunchy bangs, we blew into that store like it was our own private carnival. Bright and shiny sample-giving employees were abound, promoting everything *Bloomie's* without discrimination. We weren't exactly profiled as customers planning to drop a few grand in the fur department, but we still got a grandiose greeting from a very happy jazz-handed mime that gestured us to follow him. Of course we did, he could have been leading us to the Seventh Circle of Hell but we happily went along. Mr. Mime brought us to a cosmetic skincare counter. In front of the counter stood a beautiful, Eastern European woman smiling knowingly as if she was expecting us. Dramatically, he bid us adieu and skipped away to bake cookies in a hollow tree.

Skincare Woman: "Ehloo, voud yoo like ay hghand massaje tooday?"

Linda: "IIII wiiil. My skin's so dry I haaate it."

Skincare Woman: "Paleez seet doun in dis chayr."

Linda, with her clear, baby-soft 13-year-old face and dimpled cheek, hopped onto the stool. Immediately, the European saleswoman grabbed her hand to closely examine before squeezing a quarter-sized dollop of very expensive "crème" onto her palm.

Skincare Woman: "Zees iz a Vulgarian coompanee dat maeks exquiseet balms for dee skeen, excloosively vor da Bloomingdale-ess."

Linda: "Cool. It's nice."

Quiet and busily igniting pressure points as a perk to the already complimentary hand massage, she looked up at Linda's face.

Skincare Woman: "Yoo hgave beeuteeful skeen. Vat pdradooct do yoo yoose on yoor faes?"

Linda: "*Vaseline...*"

Vaseline. Her hydration "go-to" serves as baby rash ointment and *WD-40* in a pinch. The Euro-skincare woman's expression was a combination of disgust, envy and appreciation all rolled-up into one, well worth butchering an age-old Christmas carol to witness. I guffawed first then eventually so did the Eastern Block beauty.

It's no surprise we never got a callback from the theater, I actually think we forgot about it by the time we were seduced by the mime. Of course seeing children attack a chorus audition like their next can of beans depended on it made me wonder what the hell I was doing there, but I didn't question why I wasn't a show kid orphan. The Ghost of Christmas Present reminds us to experience more moments like 13-year-olds; before baggage from the past and anxieties about the future skew how we see ourselves. This is what I try to remind myself when I get anxious about finishing this book. Looking back, the most interesting part of that day was observing its pretenses and realities come full-circle: at the cosmetics counter, Vaseline and $200 crème slurried into a mutual appreciation for everyday absurdities. We were exactly where we should have been at the time. It wasn't at the Goodman and there it shall remain.

---

* "Send in the Clowns" by Judy Collins, 1975

CHAPTER 12

*Ship of Fools

When tossed circumstances to challenge our emotional growth, we've all made complete asses of ourselves in a variety of ways. 1. For me, immediate embarrassment feels like this gross, prickly wave of mortification coating my brain. 2. When embarrassment is realized later, it lingers in an acidic disaster located in the pit of my stomach, tucked in a trench where a piece of my pride eats crow and slowly dies. 3. There's the "I know I should feel embarrassed, but just don't" type of embarrassment. Not in a psychotic way, more in a "Hey, it happened so I'm not wasting the energy to care," way. It's my favorite (if I had to choose) and can be quite liberating. 4. Then there's the embarrassment you feel for others that resonates for years, simply because the scene was downright hilarious.

One

1995 - I lived with my parents after graduating from State University. This was not an easy task for anyone involved. I don't care how well adjusted you are or how swimmingly your family functions. It is never fun going from your first 4 years as a "legal" adult calling the shots on your every good, bad or ugly move, to feeling like an overgrown kid taking-up too much room in the nest. What's even more difficult than feeling like you're living your life in reverse is the maddening realization that suddenly your social decisions are back up for debate.

Mom: "Where are you going?"

Sharon: "I'm going out again with John Doe. To a movie."

Mom: "Oh. What movie are you seeing?"

Sharon: "I don't know yet."

Mom: "Oh. What is this John Doe like? Is he nice?"

Sharon: "Is he nice? No, he's an animal which is why I'm going out with him again."

Annoyed Mom: "Oh well I'm just asking. I'm always going to worry."

Looking back, I think "Is he nice?" was Mom code for: "Is he handsome, smart, Catholic, a doctor, lawyer, accountant, with parents still married? Does he open the car door for you? He better come to the door and not just honk. Is he honorable like Atticus Finch and does he sing like *Harry Connick Jr.?*" Although I understand that

Mom was just "momming," her concerns occasionally grew larger than she could manage.

"Roommate," from Girl College called to ask if Linda and I were interested in accompanying her two male, high school friends to a yacht party on good ol' Lake Michigan, aka a "booze cruise." This was a commonly occurring event frequented by 20-somethings from all over the area and certainly not a foreign concept to Mom. It's important to understand that Roommate was an apple cobbler, God fearing, Wisconsin snowflake kind of girl from a good, sturdy family, with whom Mom happily interacted many times. Not some goth chick who'd light her shoes on fire for sport while wearing them.

About two hours before the guys were to arrive at my parent's house to sweep us off somewhere not worth the impending debacle, I began to get ready and really didn't think twice about running my plans across Mom. She frequently used, "You are the company you keep," as her tagline to illustrate her proclamation of the undesirables in my life, so considering she knew and truly liked Roommate and her parents, how could she question the integrity of these two strangers? It didn't matter. Based on her reaction, I may have well told her I was meeting a prison escapee who I got to know when he randomly called me for an obscene phone call. "Seriously serendipity mom, it's totally fine because he didn't kill anybody, he's just lonely."

Mom: "You're WHAT???!!!"

Sharon: "Huh?"

Mom: "You have no idea who these people are!!!"

Stunned Sharon: "No…but…? What's the problem?"

Mom: "No way are you going on this booze cruise with some guy you know absolutely nothing about. Nuh uh! You'll end up in a dumpster somewhere off the Dan Ryan!"

The feud continued for what felt like a lifetime. Both our anger escalated as I frustratingly attempted to convince Mom that I did not have the judgment of a 15-year-old neutral dropping her mom's Cadillac. She needed to step-back out of principle alone, but there were no steps, only the pooling of my marbled tears despite my effort to not ruin my mascara. Crying was the tipping point to our arguments after which all logic would fly out the window; we'd yell louder and cry more as if a foolproof recipe to make our points more valid. Any solace Dad sought in the garage was interrupted when the doorbell rang. Mom and I were still busy screaming, so he had to let our mystery dates into the house. Like with most harmless male callers, he rotely offered them something to drink, asked a few introductory questions, told them I'd "be right down," then swiftly returned to the garage to polish shoes or install drywall. That is, until Mom eventually summoned him inside for more awkward conversation with people 40 years his junior. Meanwhile, Linda and Roommate's two suit-clad strangers were patiently waiting in the living room forced to listen to our muffled rage through the ceiling:

"I CAN'T beliEVE thatyoudthink NO! But, WHY CAN'T YOU Just TRUSt… (sobbing) AREYOU SERIOUS????"(Staccato sobbing from labored breathing).

.... Silence

They probably wondered if we killed each other, but Mom eventually caved. Was this divine intervention? Maybe "the louder the voice, the more the listener believes what your saying" tactic worked? I really don't know. "Fine. So can I go NOW????" My face was patchy red, nose stuffed and inflamed, eyes bloodshot and head pounding. I tried to get it together and convince myself that I did not look like I'd been in cardiac arrest for an hour. What choice did I have? The guys were waiting downstairs, I "won" the battle, and so I had to go.

I approached the top of a small staircase leading into the family room and saw my parents chatting with our dates as if what they just heard was either completely normal or a figment of their imaginations. Recovering from my emotional trauma and beyond ready to get the hell out of the house, I (dressed in a skirt) slipped on the corner of the first step, tumbled down the remaining three and landed on my ass in front of these people. That's right, the perfect end to the beginning of an evening, unbecomingly heaped at the foot of the stairs like a fresh pile of ashes. Did I rise with grace and strength like a phoenix? No, more like with apathy and depletion as Mom grabbed my wrist and pulled me up like a petulant toddler who decided to lie down in the middle of Kmart. (Those motherly instincts don't die I guess.) That hot flash of embarrassment enrobed by head for maybe 10 seconds, I stood up and said, "Sorry about that," to our savage dates, and we all left.

Two

1994 - During my State University days, there was a particular fraternity that threw an enormous annual "Reggae Party." It was always located in either a warehouse or something close to a huge, vacant barn clear out in the middle of nowhere. You'd board a bus around 7, get dropped-off wherever the street ended (usually in the middle of a cornfield), and trudged your way toward the only illuminated structure within eyeshot. As you approached the site, you'd hope to hear happy voices (not screams) and something like the all too overplayed "I Shot the Sheriff" increasing in volume, just to assure that you were on the right track. You could never be too careful as it was entirely possible to stumble into another Midwestern university's frat reggae party.

The name of the Marley cover band was not so originally named "Exodus." But in their defense, considering they catered to mid-upper-class college kids from America's heartland, they probably needed to make their brand quite obvious. Something tells me that a name like "Babylon No Mo!" or "Get jah arse to Zion" might have gone over the heads of your average Greek system's party planning committees. I walked into this massive space filled with young people, mysterious punch, nothing but time and a bus to take me home. The band was fantastic, Rastafarian flags proudly hung on the walls (not like anyone outside of the performers could have told you what Rastafarian really means), party goers donned red, yellow, green and black hats, ponchos, necklaces, you name it. As if the Rasta gear wasn't celebratory enough, somebody brought an extremely tall top hat with red and white stripes encircling the crown that could have fallen off the head of *The Cat in the Hat* himself. Well into the evening, my generous consumption of mystery punch began to get the best of me, because I was hell-bent on wearing that hat and bring my partying to a different level of asinine. Why? Too much punch? Not enough filters? Not self-conscious enough? Probably a little of everything. But hey, this kind of party called for unabated lightheartedness for all. Or at least for me it did.

It wasn't long before my drunken dream was realized and that enormous cartoonish hat found its way onto my head. I then jumped onto the stage (or maybe someone put me there) and began to play Exodus's bongos. Much like how that magic hat made Frosty the Snowman "dance around," except I was abusing someone's instrument. I remember looking out to the sea of people and thinking, "I wonder if they can hear me. I don't think they can." I'd hit the bongos with more vigor, look at the crowd and then shrug my shoulders with a, "Hey! Are ya' with me? Anyone want in?" expression on my face. I'd point to someone over there, then over there… "Hey you! No…you!" More bongos, another shrug then tossed the same expression into the crowd, "The hat? How could you not love this hat? Anyone?" I believe this process cycled a few times before my date (yes I had one) flipped me over his shoulder like a laundry bag full of wet towels and put me onto the early bus home. Thank you Jeff, I have always been grateful that you didn't allow me to continue floundering through what was left of my dignity and got my sorry ass home.

The next day, Roommate's Boyfriend (also was at Reggae fest) came over to our apartment. I was hoping the previous night faded into a shameful abyss never to be recalled by anyone ever, but no luck there. "You were eating *Lucky Charms* when we walked in last night," said Roommate's Boyfriend, "you started to talk to us, but we couldn't understand what you were saying. You were like, 'blahpfff, youfh, pgfff,' and something about losing the milk?" "I do remember that," I responded enthusiastically as if my recall would immediately reverse everything. "You literally looked retarded when you were playing those bongos last night. You'd play, and look out at us like this." He painfully imitated me in all my punched-out *Cat in the Hat* glory. There it was, that acidic, stomach-pit embarrassment flaring-up. "So, was it worse than my air guitar to *Pearl Jam* last year?" I asked. Roommate's Boyfriend just looked down and nodded "yes." Naturally I was mortified, but I laughed and appreciated his honesty. From that moment I knew, no hat next year.

Three

1988 - Fifteen isn't the most sensitive time in most people's lives, which should justify what you're about to read. I was at the local white trash mall with a couple friends doing what we did best: loitering, eating food banned in Europe and Canada and cracking jokes about the people stumbling out of an arcade we coined, "Satan's castle." I swear smoke just emanated from that place, but that was consistent with the air in the rest of the mall thanks to every other *Newport*-toting pregnant teenager and my friend Patches's (endearingly named for wearing a nicotine patch to make her addiction safer) pack-per-hour habit.

It was winter and I was wearing a hat. Not a typical knit "pom pon" ski hat but one with a more fashionable flair; a navy blue bowler hat of sorts, with a long, wool dress coat of the same color. Couldn't have exactly pulled-off the hat with a fluorescent *Spyder* ski parka now could I? Sure my outerwear channeled Mary Poppins and Ebenezer Scrooge, but I still find that look endearing. Strictly for elevation, I was standing on one of those funhouse scales that showed your weight not in pounds but in fat to thin related insults like, "What are you, a fetus? Do you travel in an envelope? Wire your jaw shut! or Try some meth man!" A group of teenage boys stricken with neglected acne, scant mustaches to match their moms' and carefully *Dippity Do-ed* mullets were walking past us. One said, "Nice hat!!" Immediately I turned to them, moved my hands through the air with rapid fire as if signing and channeled my best deaf person imitation:

"Doong may fung o meee!"

Bam! They were mortified for ridiculing a deaf person. Obviously, I wasn't. I'm still not.

Four

2001 - 'Twas summertime and I was at a bachelorette party with a motley crew of 6 high school friends and a plan to explore tacky dance bars until we took it upon ourselves to call it quits and go home. We began at a Mexican restaurant where the bride-to-be, and anyone else who was willing, drank cheap margaritas big enough for Paul Bunyan and his blue ox. I decided to take a pass on the tequila but was entertained watching others down it like Gatorade. Good ol' Patches. She could drink many a sailor under the table and all the way to his dock. By the time we left the restaurant, she was ready for Fleet Week.

We later found ourselves in an area of Chicago popular among the newly legal, convention-going or soon-to-be-married patrons. It was two blocks of loud, bright, kitschy revelry where people went strictly to drink themselves into oblivion and not for the trivia or foie gras. The 6 of us climbed a long and narrow stairway leading to a spacious disco drinkery, adorned with a generously up-lit dance floor and a few bars strung along the perimeter. Eighties music blared as we, along with about 20 other people, gathered on the dance floor to move like the white fools we were. You didn't need a drop of alcohol in your body to find the need to dance to "Come on Eileen" 5 times. This place was all about fun without judgment seeing that everybody else also looked like buffoons and didn't care. At least that's what I thought. It's not like there was an announce-ment specifying which patrons categorized themselves as uncaring buffoons.

The walls of the dance floor were lined with floor to ceiling win-dows facing the street and made the silhouettes dancing among colored lights and fake fog a lure for potential customers under 25. With 80s mainstream metal blaring, Patches was in her own universe flashing back to parties held in south Chicago's finest ne-glected forest preserves located just off the highway. Always a draw for criminals needing a quick getaway and those seeking somewhere to abandon injured Pit Bulls. This was her theme music back then and obviously still was. I found her squatting down, facing one of the huge windows while holding either side of its frame for sup-port. With smooth, agile movements typically requiring ball bear-ings, she circled her neck to the beat of the music for an impressive period. Maybe 30 seconds? I tried it one time before, it lasted a few seconds but my brain moved independently from my skull and I haven't been the same since. She appeared quite comfortable star-ring in her own music video where she didn't sing; it was like…. she had finally found home. If a Jaguar XJS magically appeared in the middle of the dance floor, she could've crushed it with some splits on the hood. Go big or go home right?

Uber-charged like they just got away with sneaking into an R rated movie, several young men gathered around Patches, as they eagerly anticipated a captivating zenith and sizzling finish. Unfortunately, all she could muster was an undramatic, 6-inch fall on her tush, followed by an awkwardly slow, backward roll. There was poor little Patches, teetering back and forth like a flipped hermit crab that just gave up. (Thankfully her intoxication relaxed her muscles enough to prevent injury.) Too bad our Patches failed her inner Tawny Kitaen in a huge way; she cheated us out of acrobatics on a car, bar, pinball machine or foosball table. I was facing a corner laughing myself to tears, when the bride-to-be found me and said, "The whole time she was doing that I thought, 'Something has got to happen, because this is just too good.' "

One through Four

2006 - As a business owner, my husband reaps the benefits of networking to grow his client base. An avid and impressive golfer, he's cultivated many connections on the course to foster both clients' portfolios and the mysterious bond that can instantly occur between golf aficionados. As much of a win-win his golf/work situation can be, even Husband found it important to branch-out and explore non-sport orientated activities. He enjoyed serving on our city's transportation committee where he worked with like-minded folks approving stop sign placement and the harrowing work of duckling crosswalk establishment. He also was a member of a very selective networking club where he met people with different careers, to whom he'd refer prospects and they to him. If he thought he was going to miss a meeting, he'd panic as if their thugs were going to crack his knees with a nine iron; a reaction he could never quite explain to me. Thinking further out-of the-box, Husband decided to tap into the cultural market and sit as a junior board member of a nonprofit art and music education organization. As much as I credited him for discovering new horizons, he was still a nice Jewish boy who loved golfing and to my embarrassment, quoting RUN DMC. Quickly, we found ourselves attending a semi-formal fundraiser for diversity in art education.

The venue was decorated beautifully, housed a generous, silent auction and the air was filled with music that was both eclectic and enlivening. As we acclimated ourselves to our assigned table and seats, we trudged through niceties and introductions, but as usual, I forgot most of the people's names within about ten seconds. I decided to preoccupy myself with my assigned banquet salad of the decade: mixed greens with pears, goat cheese and caramelized pecans. As our salad plates were cleared, a chairperson stood in the middle of the dance floor with a microphone to thank the guests for attending and "supporting" the cause of the evening. Clapping was elicited and checkbooks surfaced. Just as teachers do when students get too old to yell at, the chairperson stood still and said nothing in order to quiet the crowd and regain their attention. Reemphasizing her take on "our" children's multicultural art deficiency, she proceeded to introduce the following segment as something that could "speak for itself" much better than she could ever justify.

The room silenced as the lights over the tables dimmed and a cone-shaped spotlight shone on the floor. The deep bellowing sound of tribal drums began to soak-up the silence and crescendo to a third world celebratory explosion. Springing from out of nowhere were 3 tanned, chiseled and supernaturally pliable young men, wearing grass skirts, leafy ankle bracelets and an island glow nonexistent in the western hemisphere. Their movements indicated a lifetime of dance training from their home country. A country where dance skill determines who eats that month and "dressing up" means tying bones from your latest kill to your skirt. The audience was silent as we watched these statuesque forms glisten with every hypnotizing and seemingly effortless movement. How this was to be associated with teaching 4th graders about Mayan art I'm not sure. But you could grill a steak on their abs, so observing was entertaining enough.

When the performance ended, the boys received a standing ovation and scurried off the dance floor. For some reason, I pictured them immediately boarding a puddle jumper back to their homeland but oddly, the spotlight remained and silence ensued. Eagerly waiting for an encore, I grabbed a roll and began to pick-out all its raisins and nuts, which of course I eventually ate. Wasting good food is atrocious. It's only the dry bread part I left for disposal, plus somebody ate all the butter. Again, tribal music filled the room and out sprung 3 *different* grass skirt-clad men. They must've borrowed the skirts from the first trio, because on these guys, they fit more like tutus than flowing grass skirts. I took another bite of my raisin and watched as 3 white, doughy 30-40-somethings leaped (already sweating) onto the spotlit floor. Picture Mr. Buffo, Fozzie Bear and the Campfire Marshmallow Man, (you know the one that wears the sailor hat?), after a year of "sharing" too many of their kids' milkshakes. They moved in ways slightly resembling those of the previous dancers, but only through the eyes of the drunk and cognitively impaired. I watched them pose in symbolic stances as their inflexible bodies churned whatever hydrogenation lay under their powdery Midwestern skin. One guy's arms forcefully, as in "push through that stroke" forcefully, jutted upward toward the ceiling as if honoring his mammalian sacrifice; maybe it was the New York strip he was about to tackle when this performance was over. Their feet were planted askew for some much needed extra support and their faces were stone-cold soberly serious.

I really did not want them to be serious, I wanted to make sense of this visual assault. I tried to convince myself we were watching a satire to strengthen the artistic impact of the previous dancers. Not that juxtaposing was remotely needed but what else could it have been? Our children need this for a lifetime of diversity and tolerance right? Besides, what's another nail in the fallout shelter of cultural education? I was about to laugh as amused people do until I noticed that nobody else at the table was on the same path. Poker-faced they were, so more confused I became. I turned my head to look at Husband and found him with a beet red face, tears squirting out of half-closed slit-like eyes, slightly agape Cheshire grin and a rapidly shaking upper body. At that moment, I did not hear any noise come out of him, but the drums and Aztec death whistles were so loud it was difficult to hear. Chances are, he produced hissing sounds like someone was jumping on a leaky air mattress. "Are you laughing?" I whispered to him. The only response he could muster was an affirmative shaky head nod. Others may have thought he was seizing or at least beginning to since he was still upright, but I knew he was in DEFCON 4 of hysterics. Still holding my mutilated roll I said, "You mean they're serious?!" Another disjointed Claymation-like "yes" nod from Husband. I turned my head away from him to watch these dancing fools gyrate for about 7 seconds, confirmed that my satire theory was way off, looked back at Husband and blurted, **"What?!!!"** I dropped my roll. Now my hysterical physicality resembled his, except I dropped my head down to the table and wrapped my forearm around it, as a lame effort to hide my reaction. I had to attempt something, showing my tear-drenched face to those enjoying this *Snap, Crackle* and *Pop* meet *Soul Train*-wreck, would have just been rude. Oops, too late.

Out of pure ridicule and nothing else, our composure had of-ficially disintegrated. I ran to the bathroom to gather myself, but Husband stayed put. He didn't even bother trying to squelch his *Count Chocula* cackle that I could hear from the bathroom. We left soon after the performance, but not before taking full advantage of the dessert table by stuffing some gourmet brownies into my tiny purse for the ride home. At the time, we weren't embarrassed of our cultural break down, but we were for these guys. Whether they kicked themselves, or each other after seeing their pictures in the local paper, who knows. Either way, that performance took cajones. After that night, Husband served on the board for one more year but we never attended another event. No shock there. Now if RUN DMC were featured, we (more like he) would have been all over it. No matter how loyal a fan he is, over my dead body would a seri-ous attempt by him to recreate RUN DMC be allowed. At least in public, leave that to the originals.

---

* "Ship of Fools" by Robert Plant, 1988

CHAPTER 13

*Fake Empire

For many years, any given classroom was filled with *Jennys, Sarahs, Christophers, Jasons* and occasionally a *Tanya*, which was popular among the "down and out" set. In the not so distant past, it was generally understood that only the social elite: royalty, movie stars and descendants of old-moneyed ancestors could successfully name their kids "unique" names. By successfully, I mean, despite having a goofy name, float through childhood without regular after-school beatings for your organ lesson cash or an actual organ depending on the neighborhood.

Up until the mid 1990s, the Elites remained easily detached from mainstream society, leaving questionable television and tabloid rags as our only connection to their lives. Of course, it was natural to chat around the water cooler about the 60-year-old actress's new twins, *Uke* and *Lele*. Or why anyone would name their kid *Euthanasia* or *Coverlet*. But the Commoners were very aware of the apparently impenetrable membrane between their world and Planet Elite. We recognized this chatter for what it was: idle gossip about unrelatable people. Not an opportunity to poach a celeb name as a sorry attempt to increase your or your unborn kid's perceived coolness. Entertain the idea of naming your child *Danger?* Or maybe represent with just a picture? Like a toaster? You'd have been sent back to your mothership.

However, somewhere around 1995, the regular world was filling rapidly with uniquely named newborns to pepper your Starbucks run with baby *Mackenzie's* hungry cries, rather than baby *Lisa's*. It was no coincidence that they entered the world hand-in-hand with the "World Wide Web." Over a short period of time, its technology exponentially compounded to allow Commoners an obscene amount of access to just about anything in real time. The era of celebrities presenting themselves on their own volition as perfectly assembled enigmas was closing, along with the schism separating their reality from everybody else's. With a press of a button and 10 minutes of a staticky dial tone, the flaws of random A-listers were on a screen for our viewing: alopecia, bratty children, cellulite, psoriasis, you name it. It became much easier to identify with these people, making mainstream use of their "unique" names acceptable. It was like living your whole life eating *Spam* but then out of nowhere Easter Brunch at *The Ritz* was available for a nominal fee and a password posted on the front door.

After hypothetically receiving the green light to diversify their name portfolios, Americans took baby steps with safer "unique" names like: *Taylor, Jackson, Addison and Madison*. They were novel, well received by the public, smoothly assimilated into public school systems and easy on the ears. At one time, parents often considered the meaning behind a name before giving it to their children. Much like superstitious personality insurance should the baby fail to inherit Mom or Dad's "nice" DNA. But the popularity of trendy names continues to rise as their meanings hold less weight with each passing year:

Kieran - Little dark one
Carson - Swamp dweller
Blaise - Lisp or stutter
Blake - Pale
Rhiannon - Witch or nymph
Caillou - Pebble
Haley - Field of hay
Cecilia - Blind
Kennedy - Misshapen head
Gideon - Having a stump for a hand
Caleb - Dog or bold
Cline - Near sighted or to see like a mole
Deacon - Dusty one or servant
Wanda - To gain fat
Cassandra - She who is ignored

Hospital nurseries were swimming in: pale, dusty, swamp dwellers with misshapen heads and stumps for hands and little, dark, far-sighted dogs named Pebbles that see like moles in field of hay and ignored, blind, fat, stuttering witch nymphs. A far cry from *Brian, Edward, John, Susan, Laura* and *Dawn's*: noble, white enchantresses wearing laurels closest to wealthy doves in the rising sun of God's name in wealth and prudence.

In particular, I've always considered the name *Taylor* to be the Daniel Boone of this identification revolution; *Taylors* ran rampant in high-brow society and was one of the first to represent TV characters with seemingly regular lives. Think soap operas and teen comedies. Associated with likability and a clever stylishness, *Taylor* has become one of the most popular names given to both boys and girls to date. Oh, nobody gets caught-up in the fact that *Taylor* means, "to cut," fabric of course. But I digress, imagine a priest holding up a baby in its glorified purity and bellowing, "This is *Taylor*! She comes today to be baptized into Christ. *Taylor* means to cut!" Or during a bris when the Rabbi asks the parents to explain why they chose this name:

Parents: "Why did we choose the name? Uh, well...we just like the name."

Rabbi: "Before we get to work, please, tell the 400 of your closest friends and cousins who stand here hungry in your kitchen, how the name *Taylor* is important to your family. Quickly please, pastrami keeps for only so long."

Dad: "Well... we think that *Taylor* is...like a strong name that...uh sews God's fabric to our lives."

Rabbi: "And represents cutting the sin out of your lives too right?"

Mom: "Cutting sin sure. Is that a rusty scalpel?"

Rabbi: "Bim bom bim bim bim bom, bim bim bim bim bim bom, Shabbat Shalom!"

Now wouldn't it have been easier to explain *Oliver* which means "of the olive tree" as the "peacenik of our familial landscape?" Yes, but *Taylor* is trendy, fun and will instantly make your kid popular.

As an offshoot to this trend, traditional names suddenly had variations with creative spellings crafted from the swift throw of a dart. *Zachary* can be *Jaquerigh* or *Tzakor-ee*, *Rebecca* can be *Wrebeckah* or *Hribecka* and *Frank* can be *Fraanq* or *Phraenc*. This put reading and spelling back on a learning curve for any poor and perfectly literate sap who pronounces and spells people's names as part of his job:

Merchant: "Name Please?"

Buyer answers with name sounding like "Sharon."

Merchant: "S-h-a-r-o-n?"

Buyer: "No...."

Merchant: "S-h-a-r-r-o-n?"

Buyer: "No, C-H-E-A-R-W-R-E-N."

Merchant: "One more time please?"

Buyer: "C...H...E.A..R...(Pauses for merchant to catch up) W...R...E......N."

Merchant: "P-C-H?"

Buyer: "Uh, there's no 'P.' "

Merchant: "Last name?"

Buyer answers with name sounding like "Smith."

Merchant: "P--s--m--y--t--h--e?"

Buyer: "No. S-M-I-T-H."

Merchant: "I'm sorry, one more time?"

So when baby names couldn't seemingly get more bizarre, the Elites pushed it one step further. Come the millennium, there was little difference between giving your baby a human name and reinventing words intended to identify inanimate objects: "Oh honey, let's name the baby *Chair*. I'd like you to meet my son *Wrench*. *Areola!* Your date's here!" Why do the Elites do this? They're not Martians, is it a game for them? "Ha! Let's tell the press we're naming our kid *Microscope* and see what happens! We should start in Kentucky. They'll fall for it there!" Are these Elite children really named *Joe* and the joke's on us?

Regardless, their obscure names oozed onto our birth certificates. Technological advances, trendy Asperger's diagnoses and a bored populace oiled the Internet's gears. It quickly grew into a self-perpetuating entity spawning Facebook, Twitter and YouTube to further online anarchy. The once reliable boundaries ensuring anyone from the mailman to Santa Claus true privacy while suffering from food poisoning melted away, tripling the patchy exposure of the Elites' personal lives: the drunken starlet passed-out on the freeway; the Prince of Wherever who tripped on the beach; the pop star's nasty, one week post-pregnancy bikini picture. We've all seen them, gasped and walked away either feeling better about our own screw-ups or relating to these people more than ever. I guess for some, sharing some cyber humble pie is enough to feel comfortable naming their kids the same ridiculous words as these other idiots.

So where does that leave us? Running amok in ID anarchy? Dealing with those in the midst of identity crises unable to conceptualize themselves from fruit, verbs and colors? Is *Bob,* legally named *Rumpelstiltskin*, struggling with his transition into reality after years of searching for his Brother's Grimm, golden eggs and exactly what it is to spin straw? No. Stupid names are just names. They identify people and like every other trend, their "uniqueness" and shock value will wane. *Mesothelioma, Jenny, Nathan* and *Sock*; an all-American classroom living-out our country's melting pot moniker. Until the next questionable social wrinkle, press on.

CHAPTER 14

*Ring of Fire

"**D**o you want to go to baby Seth's bris today at 2:30?" Husband recently asked already knowing the answer. "Oh I'd love to but...I already committed to a bunny execution at 3."

I have 3 male children. Before any of them were barely a twinkle in our eyes, Husband mentioned the idea of a bris should he be blessed with any princes. "There is no way in hell there will be a bris of any kind for anyone carrying my DNA. That's what hospitals are for, scalpels belong in hospitals, not in some old man's leather pouch that he keeps in his pants," I told him. He never brought it up to me again.

Well in advance, his parents frequently inquired about the religious ceremonies (including the bris) our unconceived, assumed-to-be-Jewish children are to experience. My thoughts about publicly altering a boy's genitalia by a non-doctor on the kitchen table in the name of tradition were made clear to them every time. It's like driving to your favorite store through Grandma's old neighborhood, now #1 in the nation for summertime murders because it's "tradition," instead of taking the safer highway. It makes no sense. Everything else was either fine or negotiable:

Bubbie: "Will they be Jewish?"

Sharon: "Fine."

Bubbie: "Will they be Bar Mitzvahed?"

Sharon: "Will you pay for it? Ice sculptures are pricey these days."

Bubbie: "Of course!"

Sharon: "Fine then. But, why are we talking about this already?"

Bubbie: "Will they go to Hebrew school from kindergarten through 8th grade?"

Sharon: "No."

Bubbie: "Why?"

Sharon: "He won't be that Jewish. Ya' know like enough to wear a yamaka on a regular basis. He'll be considered a zealot and have no frien-"

Bubbie interrupts: "Can you name the first child *Azriel?* After your great, great-cousin?"

Sharon: "What? No. Who is *Azriel?*"

Bubbie: "Every boy's middle name must be the father's first name you know. It's family tradition! And you can't name a baby after somebody living. You know that right?"

Sharon: "That's good for you to remember should you choose have another child."

Bubbie: "Oh stop it. What is wrong with you?"

Bubbie again: "It's a Meitin tradition! Zadie will plotz if they don't have the same middle name!"

Zadie: "Doesn't bother me in the least. Not so sure how that started in the first place...the tradition spanned several generations beginning with my great, great-grandfather Moishenvitz..."

Bubbie to Zadie: "Ok honey that's enough already. Don't you have a geriatric poker game to get to?"

Bubbie turns to Sharon: "It makes him feel young you know."

Zadie: "Now I remember. My great, great-grandfather was wrongly accused for treason in 1900. In *July* I believe, he escaped a Kiev prison by carving a 30-foot tunnel, using nothing but his wooden leg. According to family lore, he died 3 times during the escape, but somehow came to and eventually found himself in Pittsburgh to work the watermelon harvest. Fascinating stuff. Now if you'll excuse me, the Elk's lodge has a senior's pancake event that's just waiting for me to show up."

Sharon: "Didn't *Bugs Bunny* do that once?"

Bubbie: "Pancakes! Wonderful. More calories.... See? He'll plotz if you break tradition."

Bubbie: "We'd like to host the bris should you have a boy."

Sharon: "Did you think that was just going to slip by me?"

For those of you who may not know (about 90% of the people I've ever met in the first 25 years of my life), a "bris" is an ancient, Jewish tradition where an 8-day-old boy is ceremoniously circumcised on any plank-like surface such as the kitchen island or an antique drink cart rescued from the Holocaust. This can take place at home, restaurant or any entertainment venue with refreshments after. A brief outline of events follows:

- All people aware of your 8-day-old son's birth fill your home to an uncomfortable capacity, much like an open house but without anyone leaving. The mother-hostess, whose privates are freshly traumatized, feels like a couple hoagie rolls are nesting in her underwear.
- The Moehl (pronounced "moyel"), a Jewish person trained to circumcise (that's right, not an MD, nurse or med student, it could be your high school shop teacher) quiets the crowd and discourages picking at the toffee pre-ceremony.
- Everyone gets louder as they panic to quiet-down by sundown.
- Like a retired magician asked to pull a quarter out of yet *another* ear, the Moehl formulaically explains what's about to happen to the infant boy.

- The mother, incontinent and wearing a poncho to hide her entire body, limps into the room and hands the baby to a "respected person," who then presents the baby to the crowd. I guess the "respected" can't be the mother, she's just the bitch who grew a human and is having a party 8 days later.

- Sometimes the baby is placed on the grandfather's lap for the deed, increasing the likelihood of infection. Who knows when Grandpa last washed his pants. Grandpa or whoever is chosen, sits in a chair reserved for *Elijah*, an imaginary dinner guest during Passover who leaves empty chairs in the Jewish child's imagination forever. He's the Jewish child's *Godot*.

- Standing under hot, recessed lighting and sweating profusely, the Moehl blesses the child before he removes the penile adhesions and slices the foreskin off your son. But not to worry, although contraindicated in infants, he may apply a topical anesthetic. If the Moehl happens to be physician (which is very rare because a physician would know better), he can also give a nerve block. Because nothing says "celebrate" more than an elective nerve block on 7 pounds of human who can only communicate through crying.

- Males of all ages look away in repulsion (a raw emotion that should be fully understood before considering having anything to do with a bris) toward this ancient, I repeat ancient, tradition. Pyramids are ancient too, but we still don't build those do we? No one goes to his office in a pyramid downtown.

- Mom stares while bitter tears break her composure and squirt out from the corners of her eyes. Sometimes she'll run to a different room to weep or hide in her new minivan that she hates.

- A drop of wine is placed on the baby's lips to allegedly help dull the pain. Hell, it worked for the *Lone Ranger*, why not these kids who live within 20 miles of several enormous teaching hospitals? Cowboys poured liquor on their wounds too, maybe try that next.
- More prayers are capped-off with a "Mazel Tov" to the screaming baby. The gates open for the guests to enjoy a smattering of delicious deli sandwiches, finger foods and ass-kicking desserts. This is what everybody really came for.
- The guests leave. The mother feeds the baby *Tylenol* until 2 am and pees on herself every time she bends down to pick-up one of Uncle Morris's 18 dropped plates.

According to the Bible, ceremonious circumcision symbolizes the covenant between Abraham and God, giving Jr. an "in" with the big guy upstairs. Similar to back-alley tattooing and branding for gang initiation. I'm not sure why removal of genital barrier tissue was chosen as the "go-to" for covenant representation. (I see surgical circumcision as a "go-to" to lower the risk of urinary tract infections, but whatever.) You'd think somewhere along the way, an influential Jewish scholar would have intervened:

"Oy vey iz mir, wait a minute. This can't be the best way to show our faith… yes I understand the Bible said we have to, but that was thousands of years ago…Maybe we were rash interpreting it literally. Other folks have been quite successful with more user-friendly activities: look at the "body and blood" of Mr. Christ. At the Last Supper, Jesus himself told his people this was strictly metaphorical and to represent with the bread and wine. Right? Saying "break bread" or "toss one back" would be nice, but anyway, let's symbolize Abe's pact through use of other circles: tie a red ribbon or encircle

with a washable red marker for instance. The kind that smells like fruit is nice. I say leave the circs to the Ob Gyns. We're all cousins with 90% of them anyway, how could this be wrong?"

I've always found it unnerving when supporters, especially men, dole out lame excuses to justify the bris. This could be in accordance with Jewish Mother Law, but much like enjoying a *Cutty Sark* while driving was legal in Texas, some things just have to change:

- **"It's just a little snip."**

  No, trimming your nails is just a little snip. A baby's first haircut is just a little snip. But performing a circumcision is a multi-step surgical procedure involving the following in no particular order: strapping down extremities, tearing the synechia (go ahead look it up), potentially necrotic tissue, scalpels, clamps, edema and possible infection just to name a few. Clamps? Clamps. And scalpels. Your shop teacher using clamps and scalpels in front of a wincing audience is invasively manipulating your infant's malehood. This is supposed to be celebratory? Touching even? Pit Bulls are sterilized more sanitarily.

- **"You can't see what's going on anyway unless you're up close."**

  Well hii-dee-doe. Nothing like gathering with family and friends to celebrate new life by hoping you don't see the guest of honor bleed.

- **"The baby doesn't remember anything."**

  No, because the memory is tucked into a dark place to be uncloaked later in life. It could be down the line 3 years when he eats sand, 10 years when he wants to hurt small animals, 30 years when he sleeps with his therapist or 60 years when he lets his retirement portfolio lapse.

- **"The baby experiences very little pain."**

  Really? Is that what he told you? Oh right. He can't speak and all that screaming during the "little snip" is from gas. Wait. That's to deny smiling.

We've all considered abnormal things to be normal in the name of religion or tradition. After all, up until the 1970s, it was perfectly acceptable for your so-called Catholic school teacher-nun to hang little *Maggie* on a coat hook and beat her out of envy for her future as a non-nun. It's par for the course kids, par for the course. As common as apple pie the bris is to Bubbie and Zadie, I believe they know it's archaic and can be disturbing to a newcomer, but they're just used to it.

The medical community recommends circumcision as a prudent health and hygiene practice. Three different Jewish MDs have circumcised each of my 3 sons in a hospital. Per protocol, each doctor confirmed his assignment, "You're having the circumcision done here correct?" I must have answered emphatically to elicit their non-verbal response: wide-eye contact, raised eyebrows and a double head nod implying, "I hear that sister." Why non-verbal? Doctors can't be too careful about what they say these days. Plus 50-year-old Jewish doctors may still be afraid of their mothers.

Friends, I'm here to say, it's ok to break traditions that were created during a time when it was normal to be 12 and married to your uncle. A time when the average chore for a little girl was feeding and dressing her healthy 20-year-old father. When bathing was recreational, surgical instruments were licked clean by a camel and a chicken bought you a child slave. Enough with the bris already. If not, then may your gardener do your taxes.

* "Ring of Fire" by Johnny Cash, 1963

CHAPTER 15

*The Lamb Lies Down on Broadway

In first grade Catholic school, the teacher walked our class to the church to do whatever 6-year-olds do in an empty church in the middle of a school day. I think we were preparing to make our First Confession. Great timing considering your average first-grader has at least one homicide under her belt. I remember our teacher allowing us to create our own version of the *Act of Contrition*, if we were having difficulty memorizing it by confession day. Of course we all took that one to the bank, I remember the priest having a hard time keeping a straight face during my redux: "Dear God, please forgive me, I know you love me, I'll try to do good things and be good to everybody at all times. Umm…I'll try to be betteeer, I know you love me annnd I love you too so I'lldobetterAmen."

As we walked single file into the church for "practice" one afternoon, I felt like a trespasser breaking into an unfamiliar place. Only because of simple differences like the church was dark and not packed with people for mass. Natural sunlight illuminated through the stained glass and splashed colored shapes onto the floor like giant confetti. In the middle of the aisle was a 70+ year-old Hispanic woman walking on her knees toward the altar with rosary in hand and deeply in what appeared to be, legit prayer. In my full six years of living, I had never seen or heard of anything like it. As I worked my way into the pew, I saw my teacher put her hands on the kneeling woman's shoulders and pat them as she whispered into her ear. Naturally, I wondered what she was saying: "Are you lost? Are you hurt? Did you lose something? You need to leave, these ungrateful kids have to practice washing away their sins in exchange for a makeshift prayer." But the Hispanic woman looked appreciative so it was evident my teacher shared encouraging words.

I have since learned that Catholic kneel-walking toward an altar of choice is common in Hispanic, Philippine and some Eastern European cultures as a way to humble oneself when asking or thanking God for help and blessings. For example, Mexican and Latin American "pilgrims" celebrate the Feast of our Lady Guadalupe, on December 12th by joining a procession on their knees, some for miles - M I L E S - to a location where it's believed the Virgin appeared to a few folks in the 16th century. This is not a dying art in parts of the Catholic world, but it is in ours. If ambulatory, your average American Catholic doesn't intentionally crawl *anywhere* on his or her knees without knowing an icy bucket of microbrews will be waiting at the end. In fact, your average American Catholic doesn't even attend mass every week. Forced to go to a baptism during the NFL playoffs? The Badge of Honor is expected. So given that bell curve, growing-up, my family's Catholic observance was easily above average.

During the early years, Dad usually brought Grandma to the early Sunday service. I believe she'd reward him with a sturdy Polish breakfast of bread dredged in bacon grease and homemade pound cake that she also referred to as "bread." The only difference between the two was that the former was toastable, and thus, it was called "toast bread." Toast the "cake bread" and it would've melted. Not wanting to be a widow at 40, Mom wasn't too keen on the mid-20th century, Eastern European "Hell yeah the Depression is over," diet, so Dad had to decorate it with a liturgy.

That left Mom dragging me, Brother and Sister to church every Sunday or on Saturday afternoon "to get it over with." Like most other kids, we weren't chomping at the bit to go to mass. Every week, the four of us sat in a pew while Sister in her rebellious years would sneak a few *Sucrets* into her mouth, Brother would get anxious and twitchy and I became skilled at achieving REM sleep while sitting upright. Rightfully so, it annoyed Mom how people complained about rampant impetigo and yet clamored to drink from same wine chalice. Shaking hands for "peace" after watching others forgo tissues for their hands was also a problem. So during the "sick" seasons, she'd share her sign of peace with her leather, gloved hand but slowly, as if a sweet, mentally challenged kid asked her to pet his cherished iguana. Mom contaminating her glove was a legitimate effort after all, she could have used a mannequin hand.

As Brother and I grew older, we often went together at preferred "get it over with" times. For instance: 15 minutes late after a day at the pool and standing in the back for a quick getaway during the Communion shuffle; when Brother wanted me to drive his car in circles, so he could skeetch on fresh powder from the snowstorm the night before. When we actually did attend mass, this often involved arguing with the centurion ushers who'd try to summon us to the front pew wedged between Mr. SARS and your middle school nemesis, Mary Death O'Bitchy. Sometimes Brother would escape to the school's multi-purpose room to feast on its frozen, mechanically separated Hot Dog Day stash. I still remember his hand shaking when he lifted the mushy, microwaved prion log to his mouth. I don't think he was shaking out of nervousness: maybe hunger? The microbes? Who knows. I haven't been that grossed-out since I saw him eat a hot dog at the *Amoco* station and I don't even think they sold food there.

Sister was "good" and either went with Mom or some boyfriend. Oh the "boyfriend" would happily skip off to mass with Sister, these guys made her look like darkness's high priestess. In 1985, one of them had a nervous breakdown in our basement after discovering her fresh, new perm. Again, it was 1985 and the perm was the law. I think the boyfriend vomited blood and said something like, "How could you do this to me?" or maybe it was, "How could you do this to us?" Later, Sister told me he actually vomited ketchup from lunch, but that did not make feel any better about witnessing this well-to-do, Lake Forest, 20-something's mental break over hair image. By the way, her perm rocked.

But what did I gain from all this obligatory church going? Good timing? Avoidance tactics? Hypocrisy in action? Never could I forget the image of the woman trudging down the aisle on her knees. Even at 6 years old, I felt like a great big poser compared to this person who probably spent her entire life asking for God's blessing with bloody legs. Meanwhile, a bunch of first-graders were allowed to squirrel out of memorizing the get-out-of-jail-free prayer? I had an incongruent idea of religion from that moment forward. So I ask you. "How did good old American Catholics get so religiously half-baked? Friends, how did we become Jesus's dunces?"

It's the Easter Bunny's fault. Actually, it's the fault of the American Capitalist system's exploitation of the Easter Bunny. Thousands of full moons and high tides ago, people rejected Paganism to become Christian. Fueled by political and logistical disagreements, they decided to massacre each other, split into Catholics and Protestants and primly coin it "The Reformation." All that civil mayhem over how to worship the same God. Hmmmmm. So, how on Earth did American Christians agree to accept a Pagan, as in anti-Christian, icon to represent Jesus's Resurrection? Who down the line proposed:

"Hey guys, we all dig Christ right? We no longer feel a caveman's need to execute each other over the details anymore; oh we just look back at the bloodshed and laugh. How about we all back peddle to the dark side B.C. and adopt an enormous, heathen rabbit to represent JC's comeback huh? Who's with me?"

Understand that to most observant Christians, anything "Pagan" may as well be the work of Lucifer. Pagan means pentagrams and well... new agey terminology like "solstice" and "Wicca." In fact, anything un-Jesus is typically not received well. After my first yoga class, both Mom and Sister didn't know what to make of its Hindu origin as if I was brainwashed by believers in multiple gods with multiple limbs. Why did it matter? It's not like the Hindus are exactly a riotous group, consider yoga masters and Mahatma Gandhi.

Nobody gets nervous in a dark alley running into a gang of Hindus. But back to the bunny.

Children across our nation are fed tall tales about an oversized, hyper-fertile mammal that mysteriously appears in your house to encourage tooth decay and gluttony. Let me expound on its origin. The rabbit is a symbol of the Pagan fertility goddess *Eostre* from which the word "estrogen" was derived. Each year, she ignites springtime by beaming down from the heavens and gifting the Earth her tresses adorned with flowers, birds and sunlight. She leaves behind her sparkling swirls of goddessness to stimulate viable foliage, all animal births, teenage pregnancies and other annual life revival. Lore has it that upon Eostre's late arrival one spring, she discovered a dying bird on the ground with frozen wings. Oopsie. Apparently, this bird didn't make the cut to travel in her hair. A compassionate Eostre adopted the bird as her pet and according to some versions, took the bird as her lover. Her l o v e r. This should be enough said, but there's more. Because Eostre felt guilty her tardiness left her bird-lover wingless, she turned him into a rabbit with the ability to lay rainbow colored eggs. Now, ok. If you're a GODDESS who has the ability to turn your BIRD LOVER into anything you want, choosing an egg-laying RABBIT should revoke your goddess license - period. She could've made her own Lenny Kravitz, Sting or young Al Pacino for that matter. But no. Anyway, it's believed the rabbit had numerous affairs (with what I don't know), enraging Eostre to the point where she whipped the bunny into the heavens to be trapped under foot of *Orion* the hunter. But she was a romantic at heart, so Eostre allowed her whore bunny to come to Earth one day each spring to give children his colorful eggs. Ergo the birth of the Easter egg. The End. Not sure if Eostre the goddess became

Eostre the spinster or if she carried on with an earthworm, who knows. Now there's a tale for the kids, not confusing at all being one of Christianity's most important holidays.

"You see kids, a man sized bunny sneaks into our home... no... he doesn't fall down our imaginary chimney...he walks through the front door......A key? No, magic. It uses magic to get into our house.What? I have no idea if a policeman ever saw the Easter Bunny, but you can ask during your school's Fire Prevention Week......So ask the fireman! Ok. Quiet... ready? ....Yes? So the Easter Bunny hides plastic eggs filled with candy all over the house and leaves all good little boys and girls baskets filled with even more candy. Then we go to Grandma's house to eat ham. Did Jesus eat ham? My guess is no. Uh, no lamb cake either. That's right...this is all because bad people made Jesus suffer with the sharp crown. Then he came back to life...nope, this will never happen to Grandpa....Because it's impossible. That's why."

Where's the Crucifixion in this modern explanation? The cave? The mysteriously moved rock? Not consuming a majority of this pie chart that's for sure. As if the literal interpretation of this story alone isn't controversial enough, the bunny doesn't help. I think it's safe to say that most, ok many, people who celebrate Easter know why it's celebrated. But your kids don't jump out of bed to recount the Resurrection; it's to count how many *Reese's* eggs they got compared to their siblings. It's to make sure they got ONLY black jelly beans in their baskets and that nobody bothers them when shoving dozens of sub-standard malted milk eggs in their pie holes. Your kids can't wait to get to the country club where they get another Easter basket only to be disappointed when what looked like a pink, cellophane-wrapped pile of festive goods was really a handful of cheap, carnival toys taped to a mountain of paper. It's egging-on the poor schlep sweating in the 30-year-old rabbit costume with no breathing hole, but eyes holes huge enough to see the guy's whole head through one. It's not wanting to go to Easter Vigil because it's longer than an hour and sporting your new, white, patent leather shoes and bitching because it's raining outside. For generations, American kids celebrated and continue to celebrate Easter in the same self-serving way. It's a tradition only found on our bourgeois US shores and when you're 6, it's awesome.

Meanwhile, the Jews think we're goofy for this bunny nonsense (and Santa, the elves and homes covered in thousands of tiny fire hazards), as do people from predominantly Catholic, non-superpowered nations. Particularly where walking on raw knees for God's blessing makes for a typical Sunday. There is no Easter Bunny or the like in Mexico. Oh they celebrate Easter like the sky is falling with special food, masks, elaborate decorations, big family gatherings, long masses and even parades. But it 100% acknowledges Jesus's rising without egg-laying rabbits stuck in constellations or trysts with wingless birds. The Polish, another group of Catholic heavy-hitters, bring baskets filled with eggs, sausage, vinegar, some representation of the Paschal lamb (not a cake, but a bone), bread, horseradish and a candle to their churches. The food is blessed as a gesture of hope that spring will bring them God's mercy. That's a basket of bland, symbolic food, not a pound of *Fannie May*. It is believed the Pennsylvania Dutch brought us the Easter Bunny, but it's the American post-Industrial Revolutionary spirit that brought him to life and right into *FAO Schwartz*.

On the other hand, My kids are being raised Jewish because Husband is a better Jew than I am a Catholic. But I give them Easter baskets for the fun factor and to avoid needing to dig myself out of a pit of lameness. Watching 8 cousins receive baskets of candy in the name of their Savior would be a cultural double whammy. I never said it wasn't fun. I once attempted telling the Easter Bunny myth to my oldest son, but in all honesty, I felt like an idiot so I never tried it again. Lying to a kid about fantasy rabbits only to later crush the joy of a smushy, little man with 4 rows of eyelashes? Oh yeah, that's a blast. Let me know how that goes for you. That is, if you're not busy flogging yourself after. I'll stick to, "Mom buys the candy," thanks.

It was Easter Sunday about 3 years ago. My neighbor across the street was hosting brunch for her family and after working her tail off, finally sat down to enjoy it. They were about to dig into a quiche with mimosas when they heard, "SQUAAAWWKK!!" They all paused a moment and again heard, "SQUAAAWWKKKK! SQUAWK...SQUAAAAWWK!" Suspecting the heinous sound was coming from the house next door, her husband decided to investigate. Not particularly acquainted with these people, Neighbor/Husband whipped a Frisbee into their yard to retrieve, so he could easily snoop on them in the process. What he witnessed was an entire family, including children, plucking the feathers out of a live chicken for fun and celebration. Like how some families go on a traditional hayride or play football on Thanksgiving Day: pluck, "SQUAWK" pluckpluck, "SQUAAWK!!" What the hell? What was wrong with these people?

The feather-plucking neighbors were Chinese and depending on the region, some cultures will sacrifice a chicken among other animals to communicate with their deity. When my neighbor told me this story, I assumed this had something to do with Easter. I couldn't imagine what, other than a resurrection challenge for the chicken itself, "Take this! You try to come back to life huh? Good luck once on the spit." I did some research and although I did not find anything associating bird plucking with Easter, it doesn't mean there isn't one. I did read something indicating chicken sacrifice as a way to ask a god for help with a sick relative or my favorite, *someone who hasn't been himself.* "Shit Johnny you've been bummed lately, let's go torture some fowl. God will like it and get you that G.E.D. you keep screwin' up."

Much like how bizarre baby names have become a regular ingredient in the American melting pot, the slutty, un-Easter bunny is a bouillon cube. He's not going anywhere and is a big part of American Easter. Why not toss the Ming Dynasty, non-Easter chicken sacrifices into the stew? What does it matter anyway? Forever we've diluted the "meaning of the season" to a methodology of increased sugar prices, airline fees and $100 per-head brunch tickets maintaining our Capitalist superpower status. Not that it's a bad thing, America is the "Texas" of the world and overdoing it is just how we roll. But all in all, the Easter Bunny is harmless fun for the wee ones. It just wouldn't hurt to think about those bloody knees before digging into that ham.

* "The Lamb Lies Down on Broadway" by Genesis, 1974

CHAPTER 16

*Tequila Sunrise

usband had a convention in sunny San Diego so I thought why not join him and make a trip out of it? While he was in meetings, I had no problem perusing the squeaky-clean streets and kibitzing with the nation's most Seasonal Affective Disorder-deficient homeless people. Low maintenance and easily entertained, yep that's how I roll...but only when I want to.

A couple days into the trip, we decided to explore an upper-crusty area filled with BoHo boutiques, tourist-trap markets and surf shacks. We trolled through an enormous beachfront resort that housed a lower level arcade of bourgeois chic stores selling "my kid can do that" paintings and $2,000 tiny, watermelon-shaped purses. Our canned response of, "No just looking" to their equally canned, "Is there anything I can help you with," increasingly ruffled retailers' peacock feathers; so we'd loiter a little longer then leave with empty hands. Ah, memories. Shopping just wasn't on our agenda that evening so, "What the hell, let's go to Mexico."

Husband was driving with me on the side,
we had our fill of Diego's beachside.
T'was not long before night
and timing was right,
to run for the border while it was light.

"Not to worry (said he),
I asked the front desk.
All we need is a license, don't worry the rest.
Alrighty (said I), so where do we go?
A place so enticing that one can't say 'no?'
Tijuana! (said he),
that's what it's about.
We'll take in some sights, maybe catch some fresh trout..."

I put on my new, overpriced flip-flops,
then off to Mexico within 10 minutes tops.
It was just too easy - approaching the gate,
flying over the border with barely a wait.
Zooming past checkpoint is when my heart dropped,
I looked to my left and saw many cars stopped.
For miles and miles they were stuck in delay,
to enter the States. Would they get back that day?

"Crap (thought I), What'd we get into?
Has someone been busted for hash in his shoe?"

In just a couple kilometers, we went from fancy-free explorers
to dumbasses when we realized there was just no possibility of
turning around. Who just jumped out of a plane without a
parachute huh?

"Ohhhhh my God," Husband said, "look... at.... that... line."
Th-they're waiting to go back? But isn't it easier for US citizens?" I said in denial. We both knew the answer and that we were in for a long night. We continued to drive and take in the scenery: house of ill repute, questionable people wearing colorful masks, a *Hello Kitty* "Tatu" parlor, dicey, after shady, after sketchy it was. I had no idea what to expect from Tijuana, if I did, I probably would have stuck to loitering in California. As soon as we crossed over, we drove about 2 blocks, turned the corner, drove another two blocks then suddenly saw red and blue flashers in the rear view mirror. Next came the sirens:

Husband: "Oh my God. We're being pulled over. Are you serious?"

Sharon: "What'd you do?"

Husband: "Nothing! Maybe there was 'no turn on red' I don't know. What the hell?"

We pulled over to the side of a fairly busy street and the policeman approached our window. (Please assume every "r" is rolling.)

Police: "Hola. What are joo doingk in Tijuana this even ning?"

Husband: "We are vacationing in San Diego and decided to see Tijuana."

Police: "Aaah ha-aa, how long joo stay here?"

Husband: "Maybe an hour?"

Police: "Joo rent cars in America? Jou have speshial Mehican insurances for dis car? Where are jour peepers?"

Husband: "Mehican insurance? Never heard of eet."

Like Lucy Ricardo, Husband takes on the accent of the person he's speaking with.

Police: "Please, you will excuse me?"

Policeman exits

Husband: "He can't be serious about this. If we don't get back tonight because of Mexican insurances.... I'm going to beat the guy at the hotel."

Sharon: "What does he have to do with this?"

Husband: "I don't know, maybe he should have warned us about the imaginary insurance? He wants money. You know he wants money."

Sharon: "Really? It's that bad here? Are you really giving him money? I tried that at home once... to get out of a speeding ticket. I was 20 over racing to get Boy 1 home within his nap window. It didn't work. Nice guy though."

Policeman returns

Husband holds money in lap: "Can we work this out? In a different way?"

Police: "Ooo-k leesen. I pretend to geeve joo teekits, joo geeve me mooney and we doone."

Sharon thinks: "That was unexpectedly easy."

Husband gave Officer Bandito $220 to bid us adieu and ride off into the sunset. We continued our sightseeing around the block with California as our only destination: "Like Reel" watches for sale by a 6-year-old, dicey over the counter Viagra, police tape everywhere and plenty of Gringos taking advantage of it all. Not us though, nope, we weren't looking for a "foam party" where the chance of trauma by crowbar was 1 in 5. Not in the market for horse tranquilizers, painted ladies of the night or pounds of *Oxycontin* to force feed our local middle-schoolers. All we wanted to do was get the hell out of this city that God forgot. We drove around another block until *another* cop, this time on a motorbike, cranked the lights for us to pull over yet again.

Husband looks in the rearview mirror: "You....you have got to be joking. How much money do you have?"

Sharon: "What? Again?! Seriously?...about $80."

Husband: "Give it to me. Probably not enough. &^&%^^%&^%%"

He pulled to the right like it was his job, opened his window and waited for the cop. Actually, with the cycle, helmet and boots, this guy looked a little more legit. Reminded me of a poor man's CHiPs. Only crooked and with no highway. Along came someone other than Eric Estrada or the blonde guy.

Police: "Buenos noches."

Husband holds cash by door handle: "Bue-nos No ches…"

Police: "I see joo veeseet Tijuana?"

Husband: "Trying to, but we were already stopped about 2 blocks back."

Police: "Ah. May I see jour peepers for de Mehican insurances plees?"

Sharon whispers: "Again with the papers."

Angry Husband: "No. No one told us about Mexican peeperwork or special insurances…listen. All we want is to go back to the US That's it. Maybe you can give us a break."

Police: "Oooh. Witout spesial Mehican insurances, Joo will need to come wit me, go to Mehican yudges and pay fine. Maybe go to yaaaaail…over dee niiiight…"

Hypertensive Husband: "So you're telling me, that if I don't show you nonexistent rental papers, we'll need to pay a Mehican yudge or you'll throw us in Mexican yail?"

Police: "Jes sir. And joo no want to go to Mehican yail."

I couldn't help but wonder what would have been in store for us if we were sent to the "yudge," or if there even was such a thing. Maybe our first cop was scheduled to play "yudge" that day.

Husband slightly raises hand holding cash: "How about we do this a *different way*. (He liked that line.) I'll give you something and you can give it to the judge."

Police: "Are joo bribing me sir?"

Husband & Sharon think: "%&$*K%^*%T![["

Husband: "Uh...no."

Police: "Hey pfssst, keep jour hand down man... jou bribe me sir?"

Sharon thinks: "Where is he going with this?"

I didn't have much to say during all of this.

Husband: "Weeell, since we need to pay a fine, I thought I could give *you* the money and *you* can pay the yudge for us. That way we all save time."

Police: "Oookay. I'm going to put my hand inside dee windows and joo give me money."

Almost $300 it cost us to drive around two blocks. Officer quasi-CHiPs suggested we follow him to the border and surprisingly, we took him up on it. He did lead us to the crossing and dropped us at the end of the line for our 100-minute wait.

I think a significant part of Tijuana's commerce occurs between these lanes. Leave it to the Mexican people to turn what could be a miserable experience into a party for us and an opportunity to earn extra income for them. Vendors upon vendors were selling cotton candy, tiny guitars, sombrero-wearing bobbleheads, *fanta* international food (that being American and Mexican), you name it. Never in my life have I seen this much (or any) doorway-sized Crucifix decor and Virgin Mary yard ornaments. I was astounded. In America, if people were walking up and down say, the *Kennedy Expressway* selling life-sized Crucifixes and multicultural Mary's, hell would break loose. Some Americans all too often voice their opinions when offended. A pedestrian, religious idol bazaar held on the interstate would probably not go over well. But the Mexican people are absolutely some of the world's most devout and expressive Catholics. Even if only devout in theory, such as the assassin with the *Nuestra Señora de Guadalupe* tattoo sprawled across his back. Jesus and family are dramatically celebrated so peddling glow-in-the-dark religious gear at checkpoint? Why not? The Mexican elders do not approve of Mary tattooed on assassins by the way.

After what felt like two hours, we finally reached the checkpoint. Beyond relieved to lose those traffic pirates and roll 20 feet onto home soil, we pulled up to the guard:

US Guard: "Passports please."

Husband: "Excuse me?"

US Guard: "Your passports? I need your passports."

Our voices dripped with desperation as we both explained how we were told by our trusty concierge, that only a US driver's license was needed.

US Guard: "NO. That is false. You need a passport to cross the border."

Husband was teetering on the edge of lunacy, but summoned a tiny shred of tolerance remaining from our run-in with malfeasance of the Mexican lawman. With a tired soul and yet wily eyes, he looked at the guard and said, "Please help us go home?" The guard looked at us, our licenses, at us again, our car, and then our licenses again. "Go. Have a good evening." All it took was 20 feet and 30 seconds (and $300 worth of cop bribes) for all to be right with the world. Gleaming on the right side of the road was a large, yellow "caution" sign of, not ducklings crossing Interstate 5, but a silhouetted family of 3, running like hell to illegally cross the border: "Caution! Please Do Not Strike The People Who Do Not Want to Be Seen!" First in line was Dad crouching down while running, followed by Mom in a skirt doing the same. She's dragging a little girl by her hand and apparently with a vice grip because the kid's feet do not appear to be touching the ground. Sigh. Well…I guess all was right with *our* world.

---

* "Tequila Sunrise" by Eagles, 1973

CHAPTER 17

*Space Invader

Many years ago, in an alternate universe when clocks had no hands and responsibility had no meaning, we traveled.

During this era, BC - before children and BM - before mortgage, Husband and I regularly explored what many a country's fruited plains had to offer. We had no problem journeying to new places ranging from bustling metropolises and one chicken towns to foreign turf across the pond. Our interests were similar enough to agree on trip activities. For instance, we blasted through the *Louvre* in about 45 minutes to locate the obvious masterpieces and snap their pictures; then we photographed each other imitating the poses of random statues. Maybe on the way out we'd find another priceless photo opportunity like the ubiquitous, bright, yellow "caution" sign silhouette man falling down the stairs. Were we the painfully ignorant Americans? We didn't speak much while in the *Louvre* and we weren't wearing gigantic, white *Reeboks* or high-waist pleated chinos; so despite our behavior, we could have blended with art-appreciating Europeans.

That is, until I asked for complimentary bread and "DECAF" in museum's cafe. They scoffed at me in their native tongue I tell you.

During a trip to America's Southwest, our first stop was to visit Husband's grandma in Phoenix. Excited to see us, "Nana" immediately served tiny sandwiches with bread and butter pickles on "soft wheat bread." She was always a health nut, but I didn't have the heart to tell her she was really buying "caramel colored," white bread. She poured us unrecognizable diet soda from cans found only in the refrigerators of people born before 1918; cans with either pull-off tabs or pull-up tabs that older people won't push back down because they get confused by that extra step. Normally, I'd turn down anything containing artificial sweeteners that were banned since 1980, but it didn't matter. Pushing 90 years old and with genes bordering on science fiction, she could subsist on Styrofoam. Plus Sister lived on *Tab* for many years and her eyes only slightly glow in the dark. As we ate, Nana proceeded to drag into the kitchen a huge box filled with about 30 pounds of grapefruit she picked with her bare hands that morning, in the 90-degree heat. As Husband got up to help her, "Now you sit down and eat honey, I'm just fine. This is for you to take with you to your next destination." I thanked her with all the graciousness I could muster but suggested we take only a few grapefruit or our puddle jumper to Santa Fe would never get off the ground. "Now wait a minute Sharon, you like grapefruit don't you?" Nana asked. "Yes," I responded gingerly. "You like it, so take it honey. So you'll have it. You...You'll give it away if you don't want it. Now where's my hug?" Who was I to argue with an advanced senior woman who made a hole-in-one that week and attributed her perfect health to her daily banana and crossword puzzles?

After visiting Nana's sci-fi youth cocoon, Husband and I ventured off to Santa Fe, ready to indulge our senses in authentic tapas, 90-minute massages and breathtaking scenery causing me to question why I live somewhere offering bipolar seasons and shrouded sun for 6 months. Although there was snow on the ground during our stay, the weather wasn't particularly cold, rather it offered a refreshingly balmy chill to the crisp, pristine air. We woke early one morning on our own accord, not from a large, inflatable Neptune whipped at my head (Earth at his) from hungry little hands the stork delivered years later. After a leisurely breakfast of muesli and perfectly pressed Italian coffee, we decided to go hiking. Because when on vacation, if you don't feel like working out, hiking helps you feel less lazy. After all, we were among the country's most impressive sandstone formations. Chronically beautiful from the sun's gift of color, they seamlessly graduated from gold-flecked yellow peaks to fiery, blood-orange canyons. Of course we went hiking. Given this landscape, we could have walked to the gas station and still felt like we "went hiking."

Husband wanted to embark on a specific trail that led to a for-ested area, where according to conspiracy theory, an alleged UFO crashed. Its alien occupants were supposedly captured by the US Military who proceeded to engage in its cover up. "Sure why not," I said. My only requirement was that we were close enough to civilization for someone to hear us scream if we needed to. We enthusiastically climbed root steps, attacked hills, jumped over streams and were happy to breath air that didn't result in acute asthma or finding black, soot-infused mucus on our tissues. Maybe 90 minutes into our escapade, we heard the trickle from a tempting stream or perhaps a babble from a beckoning brook. Speculating that we were approaching the UFO crash site, we continued to walk toward the sound until we came upon an arroyo halfway filled with spring water from last week's heavy rain. Enormous juniper trees enclosed the area, which provided enough warmth for feral flowering plants to appear fully bloomed. Scattered in the water were a dozen large, shiny rocks the color of graphite embedded into the earth. Their tops were peeking out of the water as if saying, "Come. Join our Druid circle."

Now, the odd part of this adventure was not its sci-fi backstory, government cover-up or even our pursuit thereof. It was that perched on about 6 of those large rocks were naked people. Not aliens, but young, naked male and female American citizens just sitting there silently in the buff. Husband and I stumbled upon this scene similarly to how *Rocky Horror Picture Show's Brad* and *Janet* ended up in *Dr. Frank N. Furter's* mansion. Love that scene. Among the perching people were a pair of sprightly young women. One had a pixie haircut and the other, long, sandy tresses segmented at her temples to form the small hair/ropes that effortlessly encircled her head. Both looked like they should have been 2 inches tall and propped on a glistening leaf dangling from a magic tree in Merlin's forest. Assuming he owned a forest. Another couple just looked like they tumbled in from a year's worth of *Dead* shows.

All eyes were on us, being the clad intruders to their extraterrestrial mini Stonehenge. "Hi," we mumbled attempting to look completely unaffected by the weirdness, like this was all routine at any park district pool or family barbecue. "Hi" they responded. I think when they realized we weren't there to arrest them for public indecency is when their attention turned back to whatever it was they weren't doing. "FRIEND," I should have said. "WE - COME - IN - PEACE. WHY - YOU - SPACE - PEOPLE - SO - NAKED?"

Our wilderness cred hinged on about 30 seconds and two choices: run the other way or feign normalcy and join the party.

We whispered to each other while acting preoccupied with our backpack:

Sharon: "What do we do"

Husband: "I don't know, what do we do?"

Sharon: "Ummm well, go in? I guess?"

Husband: "Go in? Really?"

Sharon: "Sure what the hell."

Husband: "Um...Ok."

So we did. We took off all our clothes and piled them in a neat little bundle on top of our backpack. Like someone was going to steal them? The transition from our land to their meteorite islands was beyond graceless and we certainly lacked *any* innate fusion with these people upon landing. I wish I could say I delicately pranced to my rock like a fertile doe in search of refreshment from a dewy wildflower, but I cannot. Husband sure as hell didn't slink stealthily to his rock like a Masai lion after bagging a giraffe to feed his 25 cubs. It was more like *Casper the Ghost* and *Fred Flintstone* invade *Narnia*. Nothing delicate about our moves. We had no choice but to scooch through small spaces between the elves and the *Steal Your Face* couple already hunkered-in:

Us (either - it doesn't matter): "Oops, excuse me, just need…to… get through here, um, ok thanks so much."

"Ewww."

"#@$$#@ sharp rock….**sharp rock**."

"You ok?"

"You're sweating. How is that possible?"

silent swearing

"Crap it's slippery what is this…ugh."

"Sorry. Yes over there. Do you mind? Ok thanks excuse me thanks."

End scene.

Assuming the Druids knew only English and a little kitchen Spanish, I think it would have helped if at least one of us (the other could remain silent or respond with a horn) plowed through these people while fluently speaking a foreign language. Americans expect the naked European thing. We are amazed at their chutzpah for bearing all without batting an eyelash. Naked jog in a French park? No problem, Totally natural. Topless Italian family eatery? Of course. They typically have the one-up on Americans with the stylish composure factor; no European visits Disney World and envies the sterling look of the loud, chubby middle-aged man wearing a too small t-shirt on the *Teacup* Ride. Or while taking in the Grand Canyon observes fellow onlookers and thinks, "Wow, white gym shoes with puffy socks, golf shirt, plastic poncho, how do they look so effortlessly chic?"

Before hitting our shores, the good narcissistic stuff is born in Europe: fashion, cars, vodka, perfume, cheese, plaids, grandparents.... College kids return to the states after a semester abroad and feel way cooler than before they left. They'll continue to pronounce Paris "Par-oui" or return to Iowa wearing scarves to bed and making daily frittatas for a week. I've seen it. We are humbled by the smooth, airy confidence of the au currant European, especially when it comes to their nonchalant nudity. The mystique of the foreign language could have made our entrance much cooler than our Yankee hee-haw. A tan would've helped too:

"Excuse me, is this seat taken?"

- "Entschuldigen, sie mich ist dieser platz frei?
- "Ça vous dérange si je reçois à travers?"
- "Чаму гэта так валавы тут?"

"May your hair catch fire as you sleep with headless fish."

- "Que vos cheveux prennent feu pendant que vous dormez avec des poissons sans tête."

See? Anything sounds elegant in French.

I wish I had some fantastical finish where amongst the goofiness, an ocean of darkness cloaked our circle as an eerie silence fell upon our group for an eternal moment. But I don't. I wish I could attempt to explain a celestial pull toward an unknown entity that lay beyond man's comprehension, transcended faith in God and shattered any supernatural intuition. But I can't. I wish I could describe a hovering blanket of iridescent gaseous microspheres that lifted our spirits out of our bodies to the repetition of 5 specific tones: "boo boo boo boo booooop." But no, I cannot. Not one suspicious 3-toed footprint, etching of light bulb shaped head on the face of a boulder, not a fossil, nothing.

Beside the situation itself, everything else was pretty normal. We sat there for maybe 10-15 minutes until the novelty wore off and the thought of that evening's dinner became more interesting than our ethereal motley crew. Like at a dull party, one person had to be the ringleader and leave first in order for everyone else to comfortably follow. As much as I assumed that was going to be us, *Steel Your Face* bolted first and the rest followed. The elf and pixie put their pants on one leg at a time, complained about the cold and got annoyed with their boyfriends, just like real people.

May they live long and prosper.

---

* "Space Invader" by The Pretenders, 1980

CHAPTER 18

*Sweet Child O' Mine

"**A**lways make them think you're just a little bit insane," said an audience member from *The Oprah Show* two children ago. She swore this tactic kept her kids in line. I think she should be president. No. Queen of the planet. It's never a bad idea for your kids to think you're playing Solitaire with a stripped deck, maybe they'll think twice about lighting a Roman candle in your kitchen. Maybe your son will be less likely to punch a hole through the door when you lock him outside because he hasn't showered. Or maybe your overstimulated and overtired 3-year-old won't decide to wrap up Christmas Eve by peeing on Grandma's carpet because he wanted to play "forest." Now, this "insanity" tactic can be interpreted a few ways:

One
Sometimes you have to do things that may seem insane to a fly on the wall, but are actually integral to effective parenting. Like when oxygen is limited in the cabin of an airplane, parents are supposed

to put on their own air masks before assisting their children. This is a bit unnerving when demonstrated in a video right before taking off, but eventually you realize that dead parents aren't very helpful. Consider this example:

I was outside on the balcony attached to my bedroom. Far from lounging on a chaise enjoying a *Bailey's* spiked coffee at 10 AM, I was out there with a tired looking desk and an electric sander. Over the years, my balcony had multiple functions. Other than a maintenance nuisance, it served as fireworks viewing platform. (Convincing children it's better than squatting in a damp field and driving an hour home 4 blocks away was no small feat.) It was ol' Billy's dog run when he felt, or at least imagined, the need to pee 6 times in the middle of the night and it has been the quaint, outdoor breakfast nook that never was. But given my current furniture refinishing stage, it's now a place to destroy things outside and out of the way.

It was a lovely, early September Sunday around 3 in the afternoon. Given the opportunity, rather than my usual crawl onto any cloistered horizontal surface to catch a 20 minute to 2 hour nap (depending on how well I hide), I decided to work on my desk. I had neighbors to consider, the sander was loud and produced a piercing "wwhh-hiiizzzZZzZZZZZZZZZZ," escalating in pitch with each second of sanding time. But that day, I had enough energy and a small chunk of time to use at my digression so quietude be damned. Admittedly, I felt downright liberated to revel in selfish noisy creativity. The gratification from channeling all the intensity of a Renaissance craftsman to transform something crappy, into a whole new crappy. There are no words. About 10 minutes into my sanding I heard:

Boy   2: "Mohmee?"

It's important to understand that my babysitter (my "wife") is Mexican and taught Boy 2 Spanish so efficiently, his English has an accent. He peppers his Spanglish with a Russian flair picked-up from Ms. Svetlana at the Jewish Community Center. Please assume every "r" is rolling.

Sharon: "Crap. No. &^%$ not now."

Boy   2: "Mohmee? Mohmee...vere are jou? Ohhh.. Mohmee? Can I eat preetzuls frum a leetle boul? A smull boul. Smull lieke me."

Sharon thinks: "DAMN IT!!! IT'S HIM! grrrr! This ridiculously cute and entertaining cartoonish little man with 4 rows of eyelashes...WHY IS IT SO DIFFICULT TO DO ANYTHING SHORT OF BEING EVERYONE'S BITCH???!!! OH MY GOD!!"

Impatient Boy 2: "Mohmee. Moh - MEE!"

I noticed when somebody is looking for me and I don't want to be found, like when trapped on a balcony or in my dorm's public bathroom, I do this exaggerated comic book character 180-degree turn from right to left. My inner caveperson is looking for somewhere to hide. Apparently in this case, I was hoping for a rope ladder to drop down and carry me somewhere. Anywhere. Boy 2 was a few feet from the balcony door and with the trashed desk and power tool in his plain sight, I thought I was a goner. The child can practically spot a shiny candy wrapper through a brick wall, you'd think he'd have noticed his mother panicking with an electric sander on the balcony.

Albeit, a mature parent would immediately approach their 2-year-old child and warn him about the dangers of going anywhere near a balcony or power tools without an adult. She'd happily get him the pretzels and accept that she isn't going to get back to that project any time soon. But I never claimed to be that person so I hid. Yes, I crouched down behind a dilapidated desk on the balcony and prayed my toddler wouldn't find me. I hid like a little bitch I did, I had to.

Boy 2: "Muhmee? Hmm she not here. Uh Kayee...Duddee? Vere's Duddee?"

The air was running out of my cabin. I needed space to breathe in order to take care of others without inflicting my wrath upon them later. Please let me sand my particleboard desk and then we'll both happily eat "preetzuls frum a leetle boul" together. And that's exactly what we did.

Two

In desperate situations, temporary moments of true insanity cannot be avoided and occur when heightened discipline of children is necessary. During these times, God is speaking through Mommy and *God is mad.*

I was 38 weeks pregnant with Boy 2 during a gnarly, Chicago heat wave that was killing the elderly and frying birds on asphalt. Mid-July with zero ozone was the perfect opportunity for our city's power and of course everybody's air conditioning to die for days. But I was never one of those over-heated pregnant people and before Husband forced me to adapt to A/C, I could easily go without air conditioning. Live in a 100-year-old, 500 sq. ft. studio apartment filled with uncooled, dirty, hot urban air? No problem. Well, that was then and this was later then. One particularly hellish evening during the wave, Husband insisted on sleeping in the slightly cooler and damp basement, but I chose to sleep in my bed. Sure our room is disproportionately warmer that the rest of the house in normal conditions. But I assumed the 95-degree stagnant air wouldn't bother me, even while housing a full-term human in my abdomen. My pets weren't even that stupid, I think the cat rooted herself in mud underneath Susan's deck and not on the toasty engine of someone's idling truck. About 10 minutes after retiring that night, I found myself in the basement half naked and covered in bags of ice. Whenever one melted I'd refill, but with less and less ice each time because damn it, I was running out of frozen water. I felt like both the dead beached whale and the nervous scientist trying to preserve myself for an exhibit.

The next couple days were fantastic. There still was no sign of power so why not gather with neighbors on someone's front lawn to complain in unison? Over-pregnant, disenchanted, depleted and dehydrated, I was right out there with them. Like an idiot, I announced to a group of annoyed Jewish mothers, "My back hurts."

Neighbor 1: "Cawll the Doctor."

Ms. Goldschlager: "You're going to have the baaaby today!"

Susan: "Call the Doctor and tell him you're ABSOLUTELY in labor."

Sharon: "I'm not having the baby today. Shut up."

Neighbor 1: "Cawll the Doctor!"

Ms. Goldschlager: "She won't stop folding laundry. Is her house cleaner than mine?"

Susan: "Tell him you're crowning!"

Ms. Goldschlager: "Do I look fat? She's fatter than me right?"

Convinced my neighbors were overreacting, I continued to ignore my completely tolerable contractions. Sister delivered a bunch of healthy babies, so I thought I'd give her a call. Some of her kids came out upside down and sideways, some were unbelievably long, some forced out at 43 weeks drug free and some she may have even made and delivered by herself. So I figured she'd know what to do. Sister would sooner give birth in a public pool before going to the hospital early, so I assumed she'd validate my decision to ignore mild contractions 2 weeks before my due date.

Sharon: "How do I know when to go to the hospital?"

Sister: "Um…I don't know, are you in labor?"

Sharon: "I don't know! Shouldn't you know this?!"

Sister: "When you drop to your knees in pain."

Sharon: "Ok, not there, bye."

Husband announced he was hungry so I thought it was a good idea to snag Boy 1 and go out to dinner at 4 pm. We got about halfway down the block when the worst, most debilitating pain, shot *not* from my uterus, but the back of my leg. It felt like my hamstring was folded like an accordion, held together with superglue and burned with cigarettes. For all I knew, I could have been in the midst of labor but that damn hamstring was intolerable. I made Husband immediately pullover, I busted out the door, sat on the curb and tried to stretch out the pain. Mind you, I was wearing a dress covered in blue flowers. It was borrowed and hot ok? *Armani* wasn't exactly knocking on my door to sample his resort wear. So there I was with one leg straight in the air while holding the bottom of my foot with one hand and the curb with my other hand. Meanwhile, Boy 1 kept saying, "Mommy! Mommy! What's wrong with Mommy! I'm scared! Daddy what's wrong with her!" The nervous Nelly neighbors were still outside watching this disaster.

Adding to this spectacle, Boy 1's friend's father in his truck, stopped next to us as I continued to writhe in pain and sweat in my big, blue dress. "Uh, are you ok?" Clearly there was nothing "ok" about any of this, but with clenched teeth and my fist digging into my super-spastic thigh, I said, "Oh...yeah, Just uh... just a cramp!" Doesn't everybody sit on the side of the road and scream when they get a charley horse? "OK then," he said, "let me know if I can help." He sped away - poor guy. So I called the doctor to tell him that I was having some contractions and that the baby decided to tear through my thigh.

Doctor: "How far apart are your contractions?"

Sharon: "I don't know, they're so mild I wasn't paying attention. But what about the leg?"

Doctor: "It sounds like a cramp. Why don't you wait a few hours then call me back."

I thought it made sense to go to the hospital anyway because at the very least, the emergency doctors would deal with the cramp. FYI - pregnancy lowers your IQ about 30%. Mrs. Goldschlager was to watch Boy 1 if I spontaneously went into labor. She was outside, we were camped about a quarter block from her house so I told Boy 1 to get out of the car and walk there. "Tell her we're going to the hospital," I said. "By myself?" he responded. "Yes you're 8, you can walk across the street. Now go!" He got out of the car and ran like a crazy person was chasing him. But this crazy person was still on the curb with her leg up like a cat grooming herself. Husband caught up with Boy 1 and brought him to the neighbors himself as I waited on the curb with my new friend, *Delirium*. By the time we got to the hospital, Boy 2 was born shortly after. Suffice it to say, a lower pain tolerance would've helped in assessing the significance of my contractions. But then my hamstring would've killed me first.

Three

When your or anyone else's children are annoying and/or rude, feel free to do or say whatever seemingly insane things are on your mind. Containing yourself isn't always the answer. It's ok to throw away all the dirty dishes your children refused to clean up. Right in the garbage BAM! They won't clean up their dishes? Then there will be no dishes! And break a few too. Just make sure they watch you do this. Here is a more extensive example:

Yeah the unabated joy of children is great until it annoys the hell out of you and drives you straight to the liquor store. One of Husband's perfect mother/cousins with the perfect, female child bought our 3-year-old male a plaything of the Devil himself, the "Band-in-the-Box."

Cousin: "Do you have the 'Band-in-the-Box?' "

Sharon: "No."

Cousin: "You don't? Oh you've got to get one."

Sharon: "That's kind of like saying I've got to get a box of M80s and some trick candles."

Our very own can-of-chaos landed on our doorstep a week later. Those of you who have no male spawn may be thinking, "What's the big deal?" Well, boys and girls are wired differently, like analog vs. digital. You see, girls (at that age) are analog. Their behavior tends to be smoother, predictable and less likely to go haywire. When a 3-year-old girl gets a band-in-a-can, she'll accidentally belt-out some Chopin then go draw daffodils on the sidewalk for an hour. Boys, on the other hand, are digital. They require much more energy from multiple sources to function and are extremely difficult to deal with when they break down. When a same-aged boy gets a "Band-in-a-Box," a tambourine will be another kid's collar and maracas only pepper the screams coming from the kid just swatted with the drum stick.

Their "play" is building to destroy, not to make pretty sounds.

During a play date at our house, Boy's 3-year-old buddy discovered our "Band-in-the-Box" which evidently, I did not hide well enough. He took the liberty to have at it in perfect sync with the crackling echo of my last, fraying nerve. Now, it wasn't just the seemingly innocuous, tiny cymbals bursting blood vessels in my eye with each piercing *"PING!!!"* that drove me to the ledge. The kid would not stop following me around while challenging his sensory integration. The only time he'd pause was to gasp then scream at one of the 100, common household items that inexplicably terrified him: the cat, the stairs, the color red, a flushing toilet, the basement, the cat in the basement, big shoes, wood, you name it. Then, while happily making noise and following me, he'd do this *Stevie Wonder* head sway thing that's only cool coming from a blind, musical, boy genius and downright annoying coming from this kid. Lord Almighty, I have no idea how this child got into my house.

When asked to stop, he'd only get louder and when asked to play and scream louder he would. I sat in my office chair, swiveled toward him, pointed to the "band" and said, "Hey, can I see that for a second?" "Sure," said the kid. I took the band and slammed it into the garbage can. "Oops! The band went to jail. It's time to go home."

---

* "Sweet Child O' Mine" by Guns N' Roses, 1987

CHAPTER 19

*When Doves Cry

Setting: Passover, April 30, 2016, our master bedroom, 5 pm. Husband is getting dressed, Sharon is sitting on the bed and Boy 2 with four rows of eyelashes is following Husband around the room.

Boy 2: "Daddy, why are we going to Unkie's house?"

Husband: "Because it's Passover honey."

Boy 2: "Vat is Pass *Over?*"

Husband: "It's the story of the Israelites escaping Egypt and the Pharaoh. Moses, their leader, told Pharaoh that they were going to be sent 10 plagues if he didn't let my people go…"

Sharon: "Here we go."

Boy 2: "Plagues, vat are plagues?"

SHARON T. MEITIN

Sharon: "See?"

Husband: "Plagues are bad things that happened to the Egyptians if he didn't *let my people go.*"

Sharon: "Why do you keep saying that?"

Boy2: "Vat bad things?"

Sharon: "Fantastic."

Husband: "Well, there were 10 of them and the first was God turning all the rivers into blood."

To be continued...

Note: *Typically, **"What are you thinking?"** would have flown out of my mouth and into Husband's leaky kid filter. However over the years, I've realized that early intervention isn't always the best to prevent accidental, Dad-inspired nightmares. Most likely, Boy 2 would have asked, "Vy did Mummy say, 'vat are you tinking?' like dat?" With the best of intentions, Husband would try to explain, "Mommy doesn't want you to know about the plagues because they're very scary and she thinks you'll have night terrors or see monsters in your closet."*

It's horrible. Like watching someone wax a dirty car.

I'll never forget Boy 1's first (that he didn't sleep through) Passover. Naturally Bubbie was over the moon trying to make it fun for him, but even *she* was limited. He didn't care about the dancing matzo coloring book or *Thomas the Train* yamaka, which accidentally fell in the toilet during his Yom Kippur Service bathroom break (sorry Bubbie). Her last resort was a set of The Ten Plagues finger puppets. I thought it was a joke, I really did. I thought maybe she bought them from a homeless lady sitting outside a fundraiser, like because they were so odd, she just had to get them. Nope, thankfully Boy 1 was too young to care. "Looook Tottie!!" said Bubbie as she tossed them on the table. This is what they looked like:

Blood: A piece of red, rectangular felt with eyes rolling up in its "head." It was wearing white gloves, with one "hand" on its forehead and the other on its stomach. Frowning as if sad and not evil, I didn't understand; shouldn't the blood have been smiling and happy to infect? How do you explain the sad patch of plague blood to the kids? Is the tainted blood-puddle not feeling well? The blood killed all the fish. Who's the victim here? Kids shouldn't play with anything blood related anyway.

Frogs: Just a smiling, dancing frog made out of green felt, or may-be it was hopping. Either way, the frog is happy to part of team-plague intended to gross-out humans solely by outnumbering them and being themselves. The representation is accurate enough, but frogs always seemed disproportionately tame; they didn't morph into dinosaurs and eat people, which would have made one hell of a plague *and* finger puppet. This one never belonged in my opinion.

Lice: Grey felt that looked like 3, stacked marshmallows topped with antennae, a maniacal grin and a face to put it on. Licking its lips, it was drunk with power and might as well have been flipping us off. Grey, personified marshmallow lice were still lice and disgusting. What kid wants to handle that during dinner?

"Eww... Mommy wouldn't let me go to the biggest sleepover of the year because of you!! You're supposed to die!" Lice don't have lips anyway.

Wild Animals: Like the lice, a lion was licking its lips. But lions actually have lips and are cute when not killing things. Plus they're trainable, so very doable as a plague and plaything.

Dead Cattle: Depicted (yes, with felt) as a sick and sad cartoon-like cow in bed with a thermometer in its mouth and an ice pack on its head. But the cow looked like a golden retriever and anthrax kills, ok kids? Nothing fun about a cattle plague puppet. Especially if you're serving brisket.

Boils: This infected, felt person actually looked like a beige carrot with tufts of black yarn for hair/stem and spots all over. The carrot-person's hands were on the sides of its face as if saying, "Oh no!! Boils!" wearing a t-shirt that said, "Boils." Thanks. I'm sorry, but boils, puppets and dinner should never have anything to do with each other - period.

Hail: Who decided that a clown was a dead-ringer for hail? A white oval with: big eyes, giant grin, bright orange eyebrows and matching flame-like hair. How the hell is this supposed to look like hail? It was wearing earmuffs and a scarf, can hail get too cold for itself? The most confusing and inaccurate puppet depiction of all the plagues. Hail isn't even yucky and didn't need much "cute-ifying" for puppet purposes, but someone decided it should resemble John Wayne Gacy. Good luck next time the kids hear of a hailstorm in the forecast.

Locusts: Looked like a smiling green bean with eyes, antennae and still "plagues" modern civilization. A bit too close to home, it's the Trojan Horse of plagues and the least ugly puppet. Because dang it, if we get a plague, we'd feel much better if it's as attractive as possible. That is as plagues go, we can't be plagued with kittens now can we.

Darkness: A frowning, pointy-eared elfin creature made of black felt. Where did he come from? Was this supposed to be a frightened person or frightened boogey man? They made Blood amorphous, why not darkness? If your kids were not afraid of the dark, they will be now. Thanks morons.

Slaying of First Born: Sigh. Somehow a human sacrifice finger puppet sounds wrong but why stop now? Can't sugar coat this one, so over the years (yes they've appeared again), I've seen two versions: 1. A cute felt-boy lay in bed with his tearless eyes open. Poor little Ramses, first he read *Goodnight Moon*, and now is waiting in silence, "Maybe...just maybe, the bad angel will lose my address." Little tears running down his face would have added to the impact unless he was just too terrified to cry. 2. The same exact puppet already slain, indicated by the "X"s where his eyes should've been. The bed converted to a coffin.

...Continued from beginning of chapter

Husband: "Then there were a bunch of other plagues when Pharaoh didn't 'let my people go.' And the last plague was slaying of the first born."

Sharon: "Oh God."

Boy1: "But I'm the first born!"

Husband: "But God didn't want the Angel of Death to kill the Jewish sons, so he instructed the Israelites to mark their doors with lamb's blood so he'd pass over their house. And that's why we call it Passover. So after the Pharaoh's son was slain, he 'let my people' go. But the Israelites left so quickly, they didn't have time for their bread to rise and that's how we got matzo."

Sharon: "You know this is going verbatim into the book, right?"

Being a non-Jew, I didn't know from the Angel of Death. I fell into my first introduction over 30 years ago on Easter "Eve." Thanks to pre-holiday default TV, *The Ten Commandments* playing on 3 of our 8 cableless channels bumped Dad's usual Saturday programming.

'Twas the night before Easter many moons ago.
I was hoping to catch a *Claymation* show,
about chocolaty eggs, maybe a *Peep* or two
but Dad had already been watching the tube.
Supine on the floor, hands lifting his head,
like beginning a crunch
or propped up in bed.
Uncomfortable it looked,
but it wasn't for him,
to watch hours of shows
like *Wonder Woman*,
Hogan's Heroes, Hart to Hart, Magnum PI were some,

Victory at Sea or *Patton,*
all about wars we've won.
When an unfamiliar genre graced our home screen,
I easily assumed we had company.
Once I heard football and its banter full throttle.
At home sports were rare,
like swilling beer from a bottle.
Only Dad was watching
Super Bowl '86,
observing his home team,
I guess just for kicks.
Months later I found,
Dad watching Moses,
toss around his staff,
because the burning bush proposes.

"Not much else on,
but slaves painting doors,
to say 'Yo death angel!
don't come around here no more!' "

I watched bronzed, method actors slop blood on their doorframes
and listened to Dad explain why. Even in *Technicolor*, it was a
disturbing concept, but at 13, I didn't take it much further than
that. Fast-forward 30 years, and now I have some questions.
I understand this story is straight out of *The Bible* and
epic Hollywood productions, but you can't tell me the Israelites
were happy with this lack of security. As much as my limited
ability has allowed, I've tried to put myself in their sandals and
I'm pretty sure I would have been very uncomfortable with
how this was handled:

From God via Moses, according to Moses, to the still enslaved Israelites:

"Hey guys, I spoke with God this morning and he's furious Pharaoh hasn't budged after nine, typically effective plagues. He apologizes for this mess and had decided to kick-up the plaguing to the next level for you guys ok? So, if Pharaoh doesn't change his tune by tonight, God will employ his super-natural secret force to kill every, as in Paradise to Purgatory every, Egyptian firstborn son. No exceptions or playing favorites. Even firstborn male cows are included, that's how mad he is. Speaking of animals, The Angel of Death will be doing the deed. The Banshee of Torture you've heard rumors about? Small potatoes in comparison.

So Please! Everybody listen to the following instructions:

- Find some lamb's blood. Sorry kids I know they're cute. Participating distributors are etched on this tree.
- Saturate a stick, broom or cloth.
- Smear the blood on the post above your front door - please share if you have any leftover, there's no need to be hazers about it.
- Lock yourself in your house and hope for the best.

If your door is marked properly, the Angel of Death should see the red and know to pass over your house. Remember, you are only in the clear when the Angel of Death is completely out of your properties' air space. Sorry, I have no idea what this thing looks like, but I'm sure you'll figure it out. Any questions? Ok guys, keep the faith. Oh! By the way, if some of your lamb's blood accidentally marks your Egyptian neighbors' doors, it's a 'don't ask don't tell' situation got it? This is really for the youths.

Hands in the middle everyone!!!   LET MY PEOPLE GOOOOOOYEEHH-HHHH!"

———

As if the Israelites weren't stressed enough, they had to provide landmarks to their God-given assassin. The Angel of Death was the second most powerful entity in all creation and responsible for the perpetuity of Judaism. Shouldn't it have known where it was going? A wrong turn or confusion in a cul-de-sac is unheard of for an angel right? Don't they just show up wherever clouds and lightning bolts drop them to perform miracles? Apparently not, because God sent his people a special needs intern to identify brownish, dried blood on the sides of brown houses while flying over them in the dark. How was this a good idea? I'd complain:

Amoz: "Um honey? We have an issue. By the time I got home from the inn, watched the pomegranate toss and took a nap, the lamb's blood was sold out. I checked with the neighbors, the torture chambers and the butcher. Not a drop available."

Mrs. Amoz: "You idiot! You knew tonight is 'blood night' and now everything is closed and Joshua's got to go to your mom's. You'd better hope this thing doesn't know his way to Kibroth Hattaavah!"

Amoz: "I'm so sorry I screwed-up, I promise I..."

Mrs. Amoz: "Shut up Amoz! Mazel Tov. I've never hated you as much as I do right now. Feh!!"

Later

Amoz's Friend: "Here Amoz, try this paint on your door. It should look like dried blood being a clay finish and all. Let's hope the weather prophet was wrong about the rain huh?"

Amoz: "Why is it so dark? Shouldn't it be bright red?"

Amoz's Friend: "Blood dries quickly man."

Amoz: "If my wife finds out *Binyamin Moshe's* 'Tawny Day Red' is the only thing standing between our son and God's sniper… she'll have me impaled."

Amoz's Friend: "You could try attaching red balloons to your house, like people do to their picnic baskets at the lute festival, would that count?"

Even later

The Angel of Death: "Blahfhhfjlgjhhhhhh!!!!!…. Wait. Is this the Katibi residence? What? Amoz? So sorry man, my bad. Hard left on *Fig Street*. Got it. More blood next time ok? Big, broad strokes and no chalk. Cool balloons, whose birthday?"

Unkie's Seder began around Boy 2 and 3's bedtime. Waiting for sundown is always an obstacle when tired and hungry. Plus the kids get cranky too. Auntie worked her tail off assembling an impressive spread and the table was packed with an interesting mix of people. The no-nonsense Eastern European Jews were on one side and

Auntie's Argentineans who would've loved a little Spanish guitar to lighten the mood, were on the other. Filling the gaps were Mrs. and Mr. Susan, an Italian border who lived upstairs and a couple of Unkie's strays, including a homeless guy he met on Devon Avenue the day before and the Korean waitress from his favorite eatery.

My toddler screeched like an angry baboon immediately after the explanation of the dead-lamb bone on the Seder plate. Eerily apropos wouldn't you say? Boy 2 held-up a wine goblet and yelled "YEAH, YEAH, YEAH!" during the Seder's first and most solemn toast, (I heard Uncle Jolly in that one), and Mr. Susan wore his pink baseball hat for spring. While people were getting hungrier and crankier, Unkie insisted that each person "welcome to the table (talk about) anyone alive or dead who you wish could be here tonight." This is when feisty, Argentinian Auntie warned, "Dis ees reediculus, I am gitting da food befor it gits colde." As my body continued to catabolize, a spastic knot on the back of my neck surfaced. I began to laugh for whatever reason, which only made the spasm ping-pong between my upper and mid-vertebrae and generate heat in the process. Long before it was my turn to "welcome someone to the table" who could feed me, I excused myself to the living room, hoping to find anything to sandwich between my knot and a flat surface for relief. I spotted a pile of firewood, so I took a log, put it on the floor and lay face up on its edge. Once it was good and wedged between my spine and the rest of my back, I shimmied around for about 5 minutes to work-out the knot. The non-eating part of the Seder was still in full swing, so my starving self was definitely not ready to return to the table with imaginary people. I moseyed into the kitchen and stared out the window as I ate hard-boiled eggs, sweet potatoes and dessert. I felt much better.

When my blood sugar normalized, I waited in the kitchen for everybody to finish the Seder before I returned to the table. I wanted to be respectful considering my personal Seder ended about 20 minutes earlier. As I entered the dining room, Susan stood up and attempted to open the sliding door for some air. Now, Unkie and Auntie live in an old, quaint house and sometimes old, quaint houses have old, sliding doors that haven't been functional since *Eisenhower*. I'm not sure about the science behind it, but I think if a sliding door hasn't been opened in over 50 years, it's not going to open easily, if at all. Susan used every fiber of her strength to dislodge whatever was keeping that door sealed and forced it open. I hadn't seen anything like that since college when I was out to dinner with Dad at a townie restaurant with no circulation. He was living with an undiagnosed, hyperactive thyroid, which made him an overheated mess. Deciding to open a window that was painted shut for probably 3 decades, he jammed a butter knife into the frame and successfully wedged it open.

Here's to the Exodus: my personal one to Auntie's kitchen and the ancient one that made Passover something to celebrate. Was it beginner's luck for the Angel of Death? Maybe he had to use a butter knife to get in the correct houses. What's the difference? Mazel tov Angel, everybody's still here and everybody's fed.

---

* "When Doves Cry" by Prince, 1984

CHAPTER 20

*American Pie

Man, were we stupid. Our tween years through puberty was chock-full of stupid is as stupid does moments. I mostly speak for myself but comfortably toss Jill and Linda into the stupid stew bobbing right alongside me like skinned potatoes. I believe every action serves an immediate purpose and of course, influences future actions. Like writing a book about stupid stuff. Besides, how are we supposed to understand what "smart" is without having been stupid?

One

It was about 1986 on a Saturday afternoon. My 13-year-old self was very busy sitting at home outgrowing my favorite white, with red pinstripe down the side, nylon track pants. God I loved those pants. But what I loved even more was wearing them to dance (more like move erratically) to the *Magnum PI* theme song that Brother captured on Dad's work recorder. It didn't make it to work very often. The thin and tinny audio sprayed out of this tired machine as if it functioned through sneezing fits. At the time, I thought my moves rivaled an inferno. After an attempted scissor kick, "Wow I did that?" came to my mind. I think the same 30 years later, but from a place of horror rather than awe. Buried beneath my *Nicholas Bradford* (of *Eight is Enough*) *Lego* hair was a developmentally delayed brain lobe that allowed this movement to happen. But anyway…where did I draw the stupid line? Other than on my track pants? Not at obscene phone calls, that's for sure. There was no dancing that Saturday, only the rite of passage experienced by our parents when they realized our poten-tial to be the Three Musketeer-ettes of idiocy. The phone rang and I answered:

Sharon: "Hello?"

Caller: "Hello, I just spoke with YOUR FRIEND JILL and she gave me your number. We are taking a survey on hygiene and beauty products and she said you'd be interested in participating."

Sharon: "OK."

Caller: "Great. Tell me, when you take a shower, what products do you use?"

Sharon: "Soap."

Caller: "Great. When you wash yourself, what do you wash first?"

Sharon: "My hair."

Caller: "Then what?"

Sharon: "My arms and shoulders."

Caller: "What about lower?"

Sharon: "My feet."

Caller: "OK. I don't have any more questions. Do have any names and numbers of friends who'd be interested in this survey?"

Sharon: "Sure! Linda, 555-5555."

Enter Mom

Mom: "Who was that?"

Sharon: "Some guy taking a survey on showering."

Mom: "!!!!!!!!!!!!!!!"

Once she gathered the details of our exchange, Mom immediately called Jill and Linda's parents to inform them of the wacko asking us to detail our bathing.

Sharon: "My mom called your mom about the beauty survey. What did he ask you? Was it weird?"

Linda: "No not at all. He asked me to tell him everything I wash in the shower in order...my hands, my arms, my knees, my elbows, my nose, my ears..."

Sharon: "Your nose? Like *Mr. Potato Head*."

Linda: "Totally."

Not sure what Jill told the pervert. She was probably apprehensive to share considering she perpetuated this whole thing from our end. (Only-children of single mothers are always a step ahead when realizing their stupidity.) Puberty-wise, she was far more developed than me and Linda combined. But considering she had yet to cross her armpit shaving milestone, I'm not thinking she blew his socks off. Naturally, my parents decided to trace the call. It took half a day and a semaphore but they eventually tracked our gentleman caller to the *Cook County Jail*. Well, duh. I understood the desperation behind this deviant's attempt at God knows what, but I didn't care. Why? First of all, unless he stopped at a payphone on route to his escape hatch or to deliver a salami to his cousin Domino, our pervert was already locked-up. I actually felt sorry for the slimy soul; here's a guy calling random pre-teens hoping to fulfill an *Aerosmith* video fantasy when all he got the was the *Wonka* ticket. Even if he did manage to find us, he probably would have ended it then and there for failing in his chosen criminality. He was better off in prison with his phone book.

Two

It was summer of 1989 and for no reason other than boredom, I was tooling around the neighborhood driving Mom's 85 Cadillac Deville. I decided to pull over to the side of a fairly busy street, shift into neutral and floor the gas pedal as I flipped the gear back into drive. The car jerked like it was dry heaving, delightfully screeched when rubber burned the uninspired suburban pavement, then expelled itself into traffic. That was safe. I did this repeatedly until instead of a screech, I heard a "thump." Forward and backward glided the car, reminding me of either a dead fish bobbing in a lake or that eerie calm you feel after a huge storm. So there we were, the Deville and I planted on the side of the road while I turned over the ignition again and again and waited to be eaten by coyotes. You see, other than *Inspector Gadget* and Dad, no one had cell phones allowing simultaneous access to every police dispatcher within 50 miles. So I waited because when stuck on the side of the road that's what you did. You waited for a cop to drive by or someone willing to stop at a payphone and call one. A rusty Chevy stopped next to me. "What are you doing here?" said a female voice; it was a girl from school. We were friendly enough, her daily requests for my *Throw Mama From the Train's* "Owen! You clumsy poop!" imitation spoke to her sense of humor, so I figured she'd appreciate this debacle.

She ran with a more risqué crowd, Mom described them as "tough." The kind of girls who could throw a right hook as they lit their *Newport* (guilty-ish). Their look included either feathered or huge, crunchy hair (very guilty), tight *Jordache* jeans (couldn't pull it off) and sometimes a comb in their back pockets as influenced by their older sisters. They drove barefoot and typically hanging from their rear view mirror was a roach clip won at a local "fest." I'm not referring to your typical North Shore suburban fest with organic face painting, hypoallergenic hayrides and an overload of security planted in front of the Belgium Chocolate "Shoppe." I'm talking about fests where a "broke but still works" tilt-o-whirl was the main draw. Where everyone's favorite crooked cop provided warm cans of *Old Style* to pre-teen girls and the lost soul of a former homecoming queen was trapped in a dunk tank that wouldn't "dunk" without her hearty bounce on the seat. What was the point to throwing the ball at a target when the dunkee controlled the dunking anyway? A spelling bee would have been quicker and equally effective given the struggling braincells of your average fest-goer. Oh, and the chance of a teenage boy catching his Mom and best friend making-out was high. But anyway, there was no way my parents would have allowed me to participate in such fun, so a bulk of our friendship was cultivated on school grounds. Plus, it was difficult to sneak out of my house with the motion detecting light and siren that Dad installed.

I explained my trick to Girl and half giggling like she found her little sister trying on her bra, she said, "Neutral drops? You were doing neutral drops?" She got into my driver's seat and messed around with the ignition and gears.

Sharon: "What the hell is a neutral drop?"

Girl: "Hitting the gas while in neutral, then flipping into drive."

Sharon: "Well yes then, I guess I was doing neutral drops. Nice to attach a name to it."

Girl: "How did you learn about this? You dropped the transmission you idiot."

She drove me to her house to call my parents and then returned me to the scene. I thanked her for giving enough of a flying fig to stop and help and I'm still thankful. A few years ago, I was stranded in the school parking lot during dismissal pick-up with a dead battery. I stood next to my car with its hood open as I watched SUV after SUV buzz past me. Someone finally came to my aide; she had 4 kids, a dog and worked full-time. Go figure. Dad arrived within 30 seconds:

Dad: "The transmission dropped?"

Sharon: "That's what she said."

Dad: "Who is *she?*"

Sharon: "A girl from school who stopped and drove me to her house to call you."

Dad: "What's her address?" *Click* went the pen he kept in his front pocket ready to etch numbers on a gas receipt.

I believe his segue was per Mom's instructions to look for signs of fraternization with punks from da odder side of Harlem like: empty beer cans with fang punctures through the middle or the head of a rabid bat lying on the car floor. But there were none. Little did she know I was stranded *on* da tracks from neutral dropping her Caddy and not pillaged by the carnival people.

Dad: "I assume her parents were home? Damn it, I'm really sick of you brother screwing up the cars."

Allowing the blame to transfer over to Brother's bond card was convenient. I was a little worried Dad would've eventually realized I was responsible once the guys at the shop looked at the car. But what did I know about auto diagnosis? At the mercy of the typical, teenage prefrontal cortex and self-absorption, it seemed feasible for a mechanic to tell Dad, "Yeah ya' definitely dropped your trans, ummm...I tink your daughter did it." But I went with it and even Mom bought it. There wasn't much guilt on my end; in the 1940s,

Dad's high school nickname was *Hotrod*, which by today's standards may as well be *Ho Slapper*. I assumed he'd empathize with Brother's reckless, performance testing of our cars and spare him harsh punishment. I always wondered if Dad knew the truth and arranged with Brother to accept blame with faux consequences, to avoid tension at home. Mom tended to stay out of Brother's technical difficulties but my sparks would've only caused our house to burn down. No one spoke of it since, so I let the stupid sleeping dogs lie. That is until now.

Three

Fast forward a few years to a concert held at *Alpine Valley*, an enormous ski slash golf "resort" in Wisconsin with the capacity of 37,000 people, excluding those who'd sneak in via someone's dad's duct-taped golf bag. Lawn seats ran about $30 dollars to see 3 acts: *Eric Clapton, Jimmy Cray, Stevie Ray Vaughn* (may he rest in peace) in 1990 and *Sting, Don Henley* and oddly, *Susanna* "Manic Monday" *Hoff* in 1991. Not sure how her act got in this mix, but much like a cute toddler yelling something hilarious during church, she was a refreshing addition. That was $10 to see *Eric Clapton*. Ah, the advantages we had, so of course we took advantage of them all.

This is how these concerts typically transpired:

- **Purchased:** tickets from *Ticketmaster* in the mall the millisecond they were available. Hadn't felt this cool since I hosted that *Coors Party Ball* in the woods the month before.
- **Gathered:** as many people with whom we thought we could spend 24 waking hours: Brother, friends, some girl, your friend's boyfriend and his 2 cousins visiting from Ireland, who I'll refer to as *Far* and *Away*.

- **Left at 10 am:** for the 2-hour ride to the 7 pm concert. Packed into a '79 station wagon (with out-of-state plates) Brother borrowed from a car dealer where he worked as a porter. Hoped no one forgot the TIKI torch but Brother was too lazy (or too frightened) to check the trunk.
- **Arrived:** at *Alpine Valley* around noon to set-up camp. This consisted of: an open trunk, cooler of beer skillfully hidden inside the open trunk, the TIKI torches and food purchased from a gas station compliments of Linda's step-father's "lost" *Amoco* credit card.
- **Conversation:** was interrupted by awkward pauses because nobody was drunk yet. *Far* and *Away* were probably born drunk, chatting with them didn't get farther than, "Con I dryve yu caa?"
- **Finally:** made the pilgrimage to "the lawn" and marked our territory with one of 37,000 blankets.

1990: Clapton, Vaughn, Cray Concert:

After sitting for a spell, Linda's and my short attention spans got the best of us.

Us: "We're going to take a walk."

Brother: "Okay, come back here at some point."

Us: "Okay."

That was it. That was the extent of our plan. "Call or text me," didn't exist. There was no "If I need you, I'll use this app that detects heat from your personal rate of cell division." So off we went.

AlpineValley had a very strict alcohol policy 25 years ago. In order to consume: 1. The patron must be able to hop over the 12-inch fence surrounding the 13 beer gardens or 2. Someone already in the beer garden must be willing and able to hoist the patron over the fence in the same way you would hoist a toddler out of a bathtub. Adhering to both of these rules, Linda and I watched the rest of the concert from a beer garden. But when those obnoxious, football field lights flicked-on at the end of the concert, we had to find our people. Linda was positive she could locate our spot on the lawn, but by the time we got there, it was vacant. We then followed the crowd to the equally enormous parking lot and began to search for the car. Mind you, to this day, I lose my car in the *Target* lot, so Linda was our *Magellan*.

Linda: "I remember we were parked next to a golf course."

Sharon: "Ok."

This golf course encompasses about 150 acres.

Linda: "It's here I swear. By the golf course!"

Sharon: "Ok."

We exchanged these words about 10 times and eventually we stopped looking. It was time to execute plan B: wait for our caravan to stumble upon us and entertain ourselves in the meantime. We watched *Mustang* after *Thunderbird* after *Chevy* pick-up zoom out of the lot until we spotted an RV. It wasn't moving and people were inside so we had no doubt it was well established in the gravel for the remainder of the evening. We did the logical thing when lost in a parking lot at night, we went *inside* the strange trailer, just walked right in. There were about 6 scrappy teenage males sitting on the "furniture" drinking. They looked confused and were probably wondering what the hell we were doing in their trailer. We sat down and said nothing. One of the boys uttered a few words, so again, we did what made perfect sense; we each snagged a bag of *Doritos* and bolted. I guess we were hungry and apparently they were boring. We didn't get very far since our laughing had us on the ground in hysterics. One of the trailer people chased us for about 30 feet but quickly stopped. Maybe the day's festivities caused his body to give out and retaliating for his lifted *Frito Lay* product wasn't worth dehydration. We kept walking and saw a pick-up truck with a gentleman that looked like a modern-day *Rasputin* asleep in the driver's seat. In the truck bed was a cooler that I decided to pick-up and see what was inside. I guess I was thirsty. *Rasputin* shifted, I dropped the cooler and it made a loud "CLANK" as if it landed on a chainsaw. Again, I bolted. Linda on the other hand was too busy laughing herself into a stupor over my stupid stupor. Honestly, I really didn't see what she found so funny, but she was glowing and who was I to pop that bubble? I started to eat the *Doritos* and asked, "Why are these wet?" Well, we were out of pranks. Finally, like a beacon, there was Brother, followed by Jill, *Far* and *Away* etc., beyond relieved he didn't have to go home and tell Mom, "Uh, I lost them." We aren't a huggie people, but Brother was, for 5 seconds, before we had to pile back into the car and go home. It was a quiet ride, I was on someone's lap (as usual), Brother fell asleep in Jill's lap (awkward), and someone named Joe drove home. Joe eventually became a dentist so we were in capable, sober hands. Because we all know there's no such thing as a drunk, pre-dentist.

The next morning was a little hairy. The sun was a bit too bright, our blood felt like cement chugging through our veins and our inner free birds' about-face to suburban, teenage reality deflated our egos. As an effort to shake-off the night and begin recovery, Jill, Linda and I decided to take a walk. We were assembled in our front hallway when we saw Brother slowly move his stiff body toward us. He looked like a Tin Man that couldn't bend his knees or a wood-plank man loosely held together with rusty hinges. He stopped and began cry. Not acknowledging the mysterious patch that found its way over his eye, Brother told us he just heard on the radio that a plane crash took *Stevie Ray Vaughn* from our world and we were the last to see him perform live. I've seen him cry only two times before: once when I totaled his *Chevy 442* and second, when I, "like a banshee," surprised Brother with a body slam while he was engrossed in an episode of *Twilight Zone*. (Mom used the word "banshee" like Bubbie used "hemorrhage." Together they've conjured a lovely image to describe familial challenges.) After Brother gathered himself, we asked about the patch and he told us he scratched his cornea. I was more curious as to where the skillfully applied, orbital dressing came from. I didn't recall stopping at the emergency room or a pharmacy for that matter, but we didn't ask him any more questions. I don't think he wanted to talk about it. A couple weeks ago, I asked Brother about that patch. He said the station wagon we borrowed was dirty and gritty and some of that dirt and grit managed to get into his eye and scratched his cornea. When he woke the next morning blind in one

eye is when Dad took him to the doctor. Well, I guess that's better than his usual excuse for random injuries: "I slipped and fell in
the rain." Thankfully, Dad's smart actions balanced-out Brother's
stupid ones. As for my and Linda's stupidity, there are no regrets.
We had an unobstructed view of a small piece of American pie and
luckily, a cosmic force watching over us along the way. Glad it had
a sense of humor.

---

* "American Pie" by Don McLean, 1971

THANK YOU...

Husband, Boys 1, 2, 3, Sister, Brother, Mom, Dad, Bubbie, Zadie, Auntie, Unkie, Susan, Mr. Susan, Lupe, Linda, Jill, Robyn, Artist Kelly, Editor Amy, Roy, Barry & Husband again.

SO MUCH.

Afterword/ Afterbirth/Aftermath

Sharon asked for an afterward so here goes nothing. I'm "Sister" in this scenario, which is actually the name of a character from *The Berenstain Bears* series, of which I am well acquainted. My real name is Maribeth, which for some reason, when I say it, sounds like "Meredith." I'm older by 8 years and the oldest of the kids. Sharon and I are absolutely nothing alike, to the point that if we met randomly, I don't think we'd like each other. As much as this book truly made me laugh at times, quite a bit of what I read is new to me. It's like we grew up in different families.

I must admit that her depiction of me is spot on. As a child, I was weepy and did spend a lot of time crying. Understand that this was many years before someone finally put me on Prozac - my personal wonder drug. I will happily stay on it for the rest of my days. And as much as I loved *Barbie* (admittedly, probably for a bit too long), Sharon hated her. Picture this scene: it was her 6th birthday "kid" party. Sitting on our couch like the Queen she thought she was, Sharon was surrounded by her subjects I mean friends, as she began to open her gifts. "Yay! A *Simon* game! A *Garfield* book! I think I already have this one. Oh my God, Orange *Tinkerbell* makeup!" Things were rolling along nicely until the moment she opened a *Barbie* doll and her world came to a screeching halt. Dismissively, she pushed-out, "Thanks," and tossed *Barbie* on the coffee table as if she just found a slobbery dog toy wedged between the sofa cushions. I started to get heart palpitations. Not because I was stunned by her behavior, that I was used to. It was just that...God I wanted that *Barbie*. Yes, I was 14, but this particular *Barbie* spoke to me. She wasn't a special edition, *Studio 54 Barbie* or *Malibu Barbie* with tan lines, but one wearing a towel on her head and a white, terry cloth robe. *Agoraphobic Barbie, Bipolar Barbie* or whatever her theme, was relatable to me as a young, budding depressive. In my mind, this *Barbie* had a shitty day; she wore her robe to the grocery store, went home, read *The Velveteen Rabbit* and cried herself to sleep. All she needed was a cigarette and she was a dead ringer for Brother's friend's mom. I couldn't understand how someone with the same parents could reject, not only *Barbie* in general, but this *Barbie* - the people's *Barbie*. So as she got in trouble, I grabbed my new plastic friend and claimed her as my own.

Despite our differences, Sharon has a special place in our family. She was only 19 when I got married, 23 when we adopted Girl 1 and the Godmother of my Boy 1. When he was about 3, she took him out for a day of fun. They ended up at a pet store and I'm not sure what ensued but the end result was an overwhelming fear of rabbits. Still, Sharon is a good resource for my children. Well, maybe not good but an interesting one. As "the young and fun aunt," I send the kids her way when I don't know what else to do. She's not me so there's a chance they'll listen to whatever useful advice she imparts.

It's ironic that the kid who reminds me the most of Sharon is the adopted one. When Girl 1 was little, I'd accidentally call her "Sharon" when frustrated. Also just like her Auntie, my first daughter also hated *Barbies*; someone gave her one for her 2nd birthday and she promptly chewed off the feet. Birth-daughters 2, 3 and 4 thought B was fun and we ended up with 1,000. However, I did find it disconcerting to watch Boy 2 stuff *Barbie* in the trunk of her pink car.

I now know more than I ever wanted to know about the Easter Bunny. Yes, it is stupid. But my kids would believe in anything if it meant obscene amounts of candy. One Easter, when most of them were little, I painted giant paw prints on the refrigerator, doors, etc. That terrified them. I kind of regret that now. At the same time, they seem to have grasped the meaning and importance of Easter, these are the kids who reenacted the Crucifixion - more than once. I suppose the fun in that was duct taping the skinny kid to the homemade cross and dousing him with ketchup. They never did get around to the Resurrection, they were too busy decapitating the lamb cake, eating ham and beating on each other over cheap chocolate from *WalMart*. They don't know from good chocolate, I've raised them well.

Our clan is expectantly awaiting Sharon's Boy 1 to be Bar Mitzvahed. We have never been to one and have been waiting for this since his birth. My kids want to ride in the chair. I'm grateful I/we don't have to do this, as monolingual rites of passage are difficult enough, Hebrew would have pushed me over the edge. Then again, I have an enormous problem outsourcing. Sharon, on the other hand, has outsourced not just Thanksgiving dinner, but also almost everything possible. I'm surprised she did her own pregnancies. But every yin has its yang right?

So, what do you do when you don't have anything to do? You write a book. I'm glad she did. I hope you like it as much as I did.